COLLINS GEM
CATS
a mine of information

COLLINS GEM
Chinese
ASTROLOGY
牛鼠兔
a mine of information

COLLINS GEM
Classic
BOOKS
a mine of information

COLLINS GEM
Classic
FILMS
a mine of information

COLLINS GEM
HORSES
& PONIES
a mine of information

COLLINS GEM
INSECTS
a mine of information

COLLINS GEM
KINGS &
QUEENS
a mine of information

COLLINS GEM
MUSHROOMS
& TOADSTOOLS
a mine of information

COLLINS GEM
SNAKES
a mine of information

COLLINS GEM
SPIDERS
a mine of information

COLLINS GEM
STRESS
Survival Guide
a mine of information

COLLINS GEM
TAROT
a mine of information

COLLINS GEM
ZODIAC
Types
a mine of information

COLLINS GEM

Understanding
DREAMS

The Diagram Group

HarperCollins*Publishers*

HarperCollins Publishers
PO Box, Glasgow G4 0NB

First published 1993
    Reprinted seven times
This edition published 1999

Reprint 10 9 8 7 6 5 4 3 2 1 0

© Diagram Visual Information Limited 1993

ISBN 0 00 472298 1

A Diagram book first created by Diagram Visual Information
Limited of 195 Kentish Town Road, London NW5 8SY

Printed in Italy by Amadeus S.p.A.

Introduction

Throughout history and across many different cultures, dreams and dreaming have had much importance attached to them. The Ancient Greeks and the Japanese, for example, believed dreams to be full of portents and warnings about the future. More recently in the West, Sigmund Freud and others have sought to use the interpretation of dreams as a means of unlocking the mysteries of the subconscious. *Collins Gem Understanding Dreams* describes these beliefs and various methods of dream interpretation. It also reveals how the subconscious alerts the waking mind (through dreams) to hidden conflicts, to the ways problems can be solved, and to the creative talents within us all.

Dream interpretation depends on understanding the symbolic language of dreams. A comprehensive, alphabetically arranged list of symbols – the usual and the rare – gives every dreamer the key to such an understanding. These symbols, together with a knowledge of the dreamer's situation and memories, will help to make dream interpretation easier and more revealing.

The valuable insights that are offered here ensure that *Collins Gem Understanding Dreams* will be indispensable to the dedicated interpreter of dreams.

Contents

1. Dream lore

Since time immemorial, the human race has regarded dreams as mysterious, significant and powerful. They link the aware mind, seeming to speak directly to it from our unconscious, reflecting our joys, anxieties and hopes. Many people believe that the dream world – through an understanding of its special language – can help us enrich our waking lives and lead to greater self-knowledge.

Dream interpretation has been practised throughout time by all civilizations. People have claimed that dreams are of the utmost importance, and they have tried to understand or analyse them in the light of their own beliefs and customs.

This chapter describes some of the ways in which dreams have been interpreted in several ancient and modern cultures.

BELIEFS IN ANCIENT CULTURES

The Babylonians

In Mesopotamia, the Babylonians divided ordinary dreams into 'good' ones sent by the gods, and 'bad' ones sent by demons. Their goddess of dreams, Mamu, was served by priests who tried to prevent bad dreams from coming true.

The Assyrians

Later, their conquerors, the Assyrians, believed in dreams as omens. One dream, written on a clay tablet found at Nineveh and dating from the reign of King Ashurbanipal (669–626 BC), for example, states that if a man flies repeatedly in his dreams, all that he owns will be lost. They also thought that 'bad' dreams demanded action and that if the 'demon' could be exorcised, or the dreamer understood advice given in a dream, the problem would go away.

Depicting dreams

This ancient cylinder seal depicts the Babylonian-Assyrian hero Gilgamesh, whose exploits are described in an epic poem, composed 4000 years ago, and containing the earliest known account of a series of dreams.

The Egyptians

The ancient Egyptians believed that the gods showed themselves in dreams. They also practised dream interpretation. But they thought dreams were based on real things that could not be seen or heard when the conscious mind was in control. As far back as 2000 BC, the Egyptians wrote down their dreams on papyrus. A collection of records in the British Museum, written around 1350 BC, distinguishes between 'good' and 'bad' dreams and also includes incantations for warding off the effects of unpleasant or threatening dreams.

Types of dreams The records list three main types of dreams: those in which the gods would demand some pious act, those that contained warnings (perhaps about illness) or revelations, and those that came about through ritual.

Incubating dreams Like other Near Eastern people, the Egyptians believed that dreams could serve as oracles, bringing desired messages from the gods. The best way to get the desired answer, especially in sickness, was to induce or 'incubate' dreams. (Incubate comes from the Latin *incubare*, meaning 'to lie down upon'.) To incubate dreams, Egyptians would travel to a sanctuary or shrine, such as the famous temple at Memphis. There, they slept overnight on a special 'dream bed' in the hope of receiving divine advice, comfort or healing from their dreams. Sick travellers even took potions or fasted to induce dreams.

Egyptian dream interpretations

Among the world's oldest
written records of dreams
and their meanings is an
Egyptian papyrus dating
from around 1250 BC. In it,
some 200 dreams are
described and interpreted
by the priests of Thorus,
the Egyptian god of light.

The Greeks
The distinction between 'good' and 'bad' dreams
passed on to the Greeks, as did the idea of incubating
dreams. Votive inscriptions, testifying that help had
been given in improving health, for example, can still
be found at the Shrine of Apollo at Delphi and at the
Temple of Epidaurus, which was dedicated to the cult
of Aesculapius, a revered healer. (In the *Sacred
Orations* of about AD 150, the writer Aristides claims
that in dreams he was given several strange orders, such
as to go barefoot in winter, to use emetics and even to
sacrifice one of his fingers.)

Pre-sleep rituals Before incubation, the Greeks would
carry out specific rituals by which they purified and
dedicated themselves. For two days before entering the
shrine, they had to abstain from sex, avoid eating meat,
fish or fowl and drink only water. They also had to
make a sacrificial offering of animals to the god whom
they wished to invoke through a dream. Some subjects
were taken to a statue of the god so they could be
imbued with feelings of awe before sleep. The subject
then lay down to sleep on the skin of a sacrificed
animal, sometimes beside the statue of the deity.

Healing dreams During the night, it is thought that
priests returned to the bedside of a sick dreamer,
dressed as gods, to give the patient medical treatment.
In the morning, the priest interpreted the subject's
dreams and told him how to care for his health.

Dream couriers According to Greek legend, the god
Hypnos brought sleep to mortals by touching them with
his magic wand or by fanning them with his wings.

Interpreting dreams in ancient Greece

At the Greek sacred site of Delphi a temple to the god Apollo housed the oracle, a priestess who, in a trance, uttered sounds that were interpreted as answers from Apollo to the questions of worshippers.

Hypnos's son and the god of dreams, Morpheus – aided by the messenger Hermes – then sent his dreams to the sleepers below. (Morpheus derives from the Greek *morphe*, meaning 'shape', because the god supposedly gave form to the insubstantial phantasms that are dreams.) He also sent warnings and prophecies to those who slept at shrines and temples.

Dream people The early Greeks thought that the people who inhabited their dreams lived near the Underworld. Homer, author of *The Iliad* and *The Odyssey*, said that these phantoms entered the dream world by two gates: those entering 'true' dreams (ones that come to pass) enter by the Gate of Horn, and those entering 'false' dreams (which delude) come through the Gate of Ivory.

This explanation played on two puns: the Greek for horn is *keras*, and the verb *karanoo* means 'to accomplish'; ivory in Greek is *elephas*, and the word *elephairo* means 'to cheat with empty hopes'.

Prophetic dreams Aristotle, the ancient Greek thinker, had a rather different approach to dreams, however. He thought premonitory dreams of sickness, for instance, could be caused by the dreamer's unconscious recognition of the symptoms. He also thought the dreamer might act unconsciously to bring about the dreamed event.

The Romans

They believed strongly that it was necessary to find out the wishes of the gods. The Emperor Augustus, indeed, ruled that anyone who had a dream about the state must proclaim it in the marketplace.

Dream interpretation In the second century AD, Artemidorus wrote down all he knew of dream interpretation from the records of the Greeks, Assyrians and Egyptians in a book called *Oneirocritica* (meaning 'Interpreter of Dreams'), which was used as a source by authors right up to the 18th century.

Guardians of dreams and death

Ancient Greeks believed that sleep was governed by Hypnos, the god of sleep, who was the brother of Thanatos, god of death, and the father of Morpheus, god of dreams. Hypnos brings sleep with the touch of his wand or the beat of his wings.

The Hebrews

Godly dreams Dreams were part of the religious culture of the ancient Hebrews. Being monotheistic, however, they believed that dreams were the voice of one god alone. 'For God speaketh once, yea twice, yet man perceiveth it not. In a dream, in a vision of the night when deep sleep falleth upon men slumbering upon their bed, then He openeth their ears and sealeth in their instructions' (Job 33:14–16). The Hebrews also distinguished between 'good' dreams and 'bad' ones, brought by evil spirits.

Incubating dreams Nevertheless, they, too, incubated dreams in order to receive divine revelation. The Hebrew prophet Samuel – who rallied the Israelites after their defeat by the Philistines – used to 'lay down and sleep in the temple at Shiloh before the Ark and receive the word of the Lord'. King Solomon (c. 970–930 BC) too followed custom by going to a high place to offer a sacrifice to God. There 'the Lord appeared to Solomon in a dream by night: and God said, "Ask what I shall give thee".'

Prophetic dreams In one of the most famous of biblical dreams – that of Jacob's Ladder – the Hebrew patriarch dreamt of a ladder 'set up on the earth, and the top of it reached to heaven: and behold the angels of God ascending and descending on it.' At the top of the ladder stood God, who made a historic promise to Jacob that the land of Israel would belong forever to the Jewish people.

Another biblical dream needed an interpreter. When the Egyptian pharaoh dreamt of seven fat and seven lean 'kine' (cows), he called for all the magicians of Egypt, but they were unable to guess its meaning. He then sent for Joseph, known for his interpreting skills, whose answer was that seven years of plenty would be followed by seven years of famine. It was Joseph too who read into his own dream of sheaves bowing down to him his future as a great man – he probably recognized his own abilities and ambition.

Forecasting future events

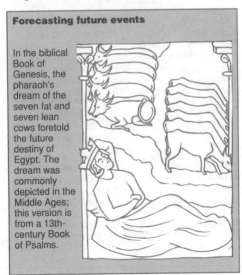

In the biblical Book of Genesis, the pharaoh's dream of the seven fat and seven lean cows foretold the future destiny of Egypt. The dream was commonly depicted in the Middle Ages; this version is from a 13th-century Book of Psalms.

Reading dreams in ancient cultures

Pot	**Tree**

Egyptian
Filling a pot was a bad omen, denoting pain. Beer poured from a pot augured a robbery.

Sitting in a tree was a sign that troubles could be overcome.

Assyrian
The gift of an empty pot augured poverty, while a full goblet denoted children and fame.

Cutting down date palm trees denoted a solution to the dreamer's problems.

Greek
Wine poured from pots indicated serenity. Drinking a cup dry was lucky.

Trees for making ships were an unlucky sign, except for carpenters and seamen.

Hebrew
Cooking pots denoted peace and domestic calm.

Palm trees were a sign that the dreamer would incur punishment for past sins.

Snake

Bird

Snake	Bird
Snakes were a good omen, indicating that the dreamer would soon settle some dispute.	Catching birds augured the loss of something precious.
Seizing a snake was a sign that the dreamer would receive protection from angels.	Meeting a bird signified the return of lost property.
Snakes were ill omens, harbingers of illness and enemies. A powerful snake made things worse.	Different birds symbolized kinds of people: eagles were rulers; wild pigeons were immoral women.
Snakes promised a secure livelihood; a snake bite meant a doubled income.	Birds were good omens, except owls, which brought bad luck.

BELIEFS IN NON-WESTERN CULTURES
The Hindus

Prophetic dreams Interpreting dreams was valued in ancient India. The *Artharva-Veda*, dating from c. 1000 BC, includes dream interpretation as well as reference to premonitory dreams. It observes that the time when a prophetic dream occurs may indicate when the event will take place. If a dream occurs near dawn, the event will happen sooner than one foretold in an early night dream.

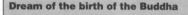

Dream of the birth of the Buddha

This relief from the 2nd century BC illustrates the legend that the Buddha appeared before birth in a dream to his mother in the form of an elephant.

The Japanese

Shrines for incubating dreams also existed (and still do) in the Far East. Japanese emperors, searching for solutions to political problems, incubated their dreams at a Shinto temple at Usa on the southern island of Kyushu. The emperor's palace also contained a 'dream-hall', with an incubation bed made of polished stone.

The Muslims

In Mohammed's sacred book, a distinction is made between true dreams, coming from God, and false ones. Certain rituals are advised to create good dreams and defend against the effects of bad ones. Later, Muslim dream interpretation became associated with astrology.

The Australian Aborigines

Some of the most elaborate beliefs relating to dreams are held by the Aborigines. The heart of their mythology about the Creation centres on 'Dreamtime', an ancient time when spirits sleeping underground arose and wandered across the earth singing the names of everything they passed, shaping the landscape, making humans and teaching them the art of survival, before subsiding once more into sleep.

The North American Indians

Many Indian tribes believe that dreams reveal the hidden wishes of the soul. It would be the most vivid dreamer who would be chosen as medicine man. The Iroquois would try to make the desires come true by acting them out. The Huron believed that the soul may be satisfied by expressing its desire in a dream.

2. The unconscious mind

Hidden beneath the conscious mind of every person lies the unconscious. It is an area of the human psyche that has a profound effect on dreams – and, it is believed, on all human thought and action. In modern times, it has only been through psychoanalysis and the study of dreams that the role of the unconscious has begun to be recognized. An alternative method of investigating dreams is through seeking a physiological reason for the need to dream.

Consciousness and unconsciousness

No one knows precisely what consciousness is or which part of the brain it is located in. Many theories have been formulated over hundreds of years. Modern thinking suggests that it resides in a group of cells in the brainstem, which connects the spinal cord with the brain. This group of cells has been compared to the power supply to a computer: without it the equipment is useless.

Consciousness is not a simple state, but has many 'layers'. Even when wide awake, we are not equally aware of everything around us or of our own actions. An experienced driver, for example, need not concentrate in order to change gear.

Similarly, unconsciousness does not imply complete inactivity. During sleep our brains are very active. Material from the unconscious can surface in sleep in the form of dreams and in waking life as sudden inspirations or accidental 'slips of the tongue'.

THE ANATOMY OF CONSCIOUSNESS
The sources of dreams

Medieval investigations into human anatomy led to enquiries about where consciousness resides and which part of the brain produces dreams. The French philosopher René Descartes proposed that the body is little more than a machine and that consciousness (the soul) dwells in the pineal gland. Although eventually proved wrong, his theory spurred much important research.

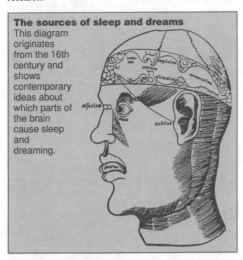

The sources of sleep and dreams
This diagram originates from the 16th century and shows contemporary ideas about which parts of the brain cause sleep and dreaming.

What is sleep?

Sleep is an active process in which the body repairs itself, and the brain 'processes' the day's events and helps sort them.

Every night, we experience four or five sleep cycles, which are made up of various stages or kinds of sleep. Each has its own unique characteristics, and is designed to maintain health and prepare us for a new day.

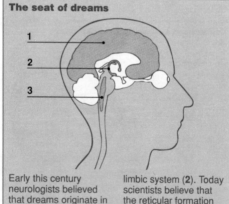

The seat of dreams

Early this century neurologists believed that dreams originate in the cerebrum (1). Later this view was revised; dreams were then thought to reside in the limbic system (2). Today scientists believe that the reticular formation (3), a group of cells in the brainstem, is where dreams originate.

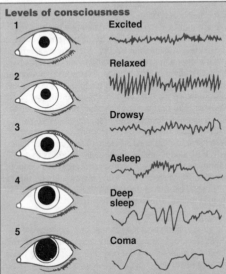

Levels of consciousness

1 Excited

2 Relaxed

3 Drowsy

4 Asleep

5 Deep sleep

Coma

The size of the pupils is an indication of different levels of consciousness. (**1**) shows the pupil in normal consciousness. In (**2**) there is some dilation, indicating mild anaesthesia. The remainder (**3–5**) show deepening anaesthesia.
Electroencephalographs are used to record electrical activity in the brain and to produce tracings of this activity, as shown above.

SLEEP AND CONSCIOUSNESS

How much sleep?

The amount of sleep needed to maintain health varies
from individual to individual. Some newborn babies
spend 80% of their time asleep; others are awake for
much longer. On average it is about half and half. By
the age of three to five months, babies need less sleep,
and the requirement continues to decrease throughout
life. Someone needing eight hours in middle age is
likely to need only seven when they reach old age. At
the same time, the amount of rapid eye movement
(REM) sleep, during which dreaming occurs, also
decreases. In infants REM sleep makes up more than
half of all sleep – although evidence suggests that
infants do not necessarily dream during REM sleep. In
an adult, REM sleep makes up only around one-third of
all sleep. The lowest proportion of REM to non-REM
sleep is among 14–18 year-olds.

Duration of sleep

The duration of sleep also changes as people grow
older. Newborn infants alternate hour-long periods of
sleep and wakefulness. At one year old, sleeping times
become fewer and longer. Instead of a 60-minute cycle,
the pattern is of 90 minutes of sleep followed by 90
minutes of wakefulness. Gradually the waking periods
in this 90-minute cycle are replaced with light sleep, so
that the child sleeps throughout the night and has fewer
daytime naps. By the age of 10, most people need
between nine and 12 hours sleep per night. The average
for most adults is between seven and eight and a half
hours. Some adults need as little as six hours, while

Duration of sleep

The duration and frequency of sleep periods are shown in the shaded areas below for various ages.

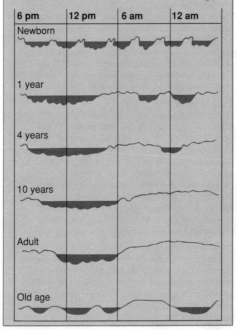

others require as much as nine. In general, a pattern of decreasing sleep needs continues until old age when a more interrupted, infant-like pattern may re-emerge.

The need for sleep

The average person in the course of a lifetime will spend around 20 years asleep and experience at least 300,000 dreams. Sleeping and dreaming are active functions of the nervous system. Yet scientists are still uncertain about just why we need to sleep at all. Theories have ranged from the pressure of blood on the brain to the need of brain cells to restore themselves.

Lack of sleep

People die more quickly from lack of sleep than they do from lack of food. A person kept awake for long periods becomes increasingly disorientated, starts hallucinating and after about 10 days of total sleep deprivation usually dies. Many people, however, have survived years with little sleep. It has been demonstrated that both dreaming sleep and non-dreaming sleep are necessary to maintain health and vitality. Experimental subjects who were woken repeatedly at the onset of REM sleep rapidly deteriorated and showed signs of becoming ill.

Physiological changes

It is not known what triggers off sleep. Different theories suggest that it is prompted by less oxygen reaching the brain; a reduction in the number of impulses reaching the conscious centres; a chemical process in the brain, probably involving serotonin, a sleep-related hormone that affects the part of the brain responsible for consciousness; or the repeated promptings of a conditioned response. During the first two to three hours of sleep, the electrical waves given off by the brain are at their largest and slowest. Sleepers woken up during this stage of sleep report that they can recall what they were thinking in their sleep, although these memories are often fragmented and confused.

SLEEP PATTERNS AND DREAMS

In 1953, sleep researchers at the Department of Physiology at the University of Chicago made two historic discoveries. One showed the cyclical sleep pattern in which the sleeper passes through several stages of sleep – from light to deep, and back again, several times. Every person has a natural rhythm of sleeping and waking based on an individual daily, or circadian, rhythm throughout 24 hours. Biological variations – in body temperature, heart rate and blood pressure – also affect the body. The sleeper is still aware of aspects of the surroundings, however, such as noises and changes in temperature, and some parts of the brain and body are less affected than others. In the early stages of sleep, known as the hypnogogic state, the conscious mind slips in and out of sleep. Often, at this time, the sleeper jerks awake on seeming to have suddenly fallen. This is a common illusion, and has nothing to do with dreaming.

Stages of sleep

Sleep involves four distinct stages that combine to form
the sleep cycle. During the first stage the individual
relaxes and drifts between sleeping and waking. In the
second stage the person can be woken by even slight
disturbances. The eyes roll from side to side. During
stage three the body is greatly relaxed and only a loud
disturbance could wake the person up. These three
stages together take about 20 minutes. In stage four the
body's tissues are repaired with the aid of growth
hormone. After stage four the cycle goes into reverse
but instead of waking up after stage one the person
enters REM sleep (see below) and begins to dream. The
cycle from stage one to four and back takes between 90
and 100 minutes. In the course of a night's sleep this
cycle repeats itself between four and five times.

REM – rapid eye movements

The Chicago researchers also noticed that periods of
light sleep were accompanied by rapid eye movements,
or REMs, behind closed lids. Electrodes placed around
the eyes detected electrical activity when the eyes
moved. By waking sleepers exhibiting REM, it was
found that most dreams took place during this state.
Other research has shown that during REM sleep, the
major muscles of the body are effectively paralysed.
This prevents the body from moving while dreaming.
This is probably a natural mechanism to prevent the
body injuring itself by making sudden, violent or
uncontrolled movements while dreaming.

Sleep laboratories

Brain waves can be recorded through electrodes placed on the head, the waves are registered as tracings by an electroencephalograph (EEG) machine.

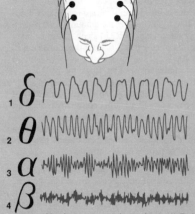

Four types of brain wave are shown here. 1) Delta, associated with sleep and infancy. 2) Theta, associated with mental illness. 3) Alpha, common when the mind is at rest. 4) Beta, found in adults and associated with perception and movement.

Laboratory dreaming

In 'sleep laboratories', volunteers are woken in the middle of their dream states in order to describe the dreams they have just been experiencing.

REM and non-REM sleep About 90 minutes into sleep, the first period of REM sleep occurs. Dream periods normally last 5 or 10 minutes (the old myth that dreams are over in a flash is not correct). If sleeping periods are reduced over a period the sleeper will adjust, first by increasing the amount of deep sleep and reducing the amount of REM sleep. Later the body returns to normal periods of both types of sleep. If REM sleep is cut short, for example, by excessive amounts of alcohol or other drugs, the body compensates by increasing the ratio of REM sleep to deep sleep. If a sleeper is deliberately denied REM sleep, he or she will attempt continually to increase the amount of time in REM sleep.

The sleep cycles of a baby last about 60 minutes, and of an adult 90 minutes. Those of the elderly return to the same kind of pattern as the infant's.

Physiological activity during REMs Changes occur in levels of hormones and chemicals, and the body displays irregular pulse and breathing rates. Men have erections throughout the REM stage, suggesting there may be a link between sexuality and dreams.

Quality of dreaming Not all dreaming takes place during REM sleep. About half the volunteers woken during non-REM sleep report having dreams, but these are usually quite different from REM dreams. Where REM dreams are full of action and very vivid, most non-REM dreams seem to be shorter, less dramatic, more blurred and shadowy, but often more convincing. More and longer dreams occur towards the normal end of sleep.

Dreaming positions
Laboratory cameras record the various postures adopted during an ordinary night's sleep.

When we dream

Here are shown the stages of sleep during which most dreams occur.

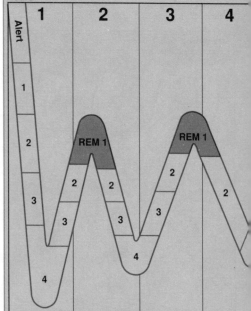

Hours

The average duration of sleep is shown in hours, from left to right. The stages of sleep are numbered vertically, from 1 to 4.

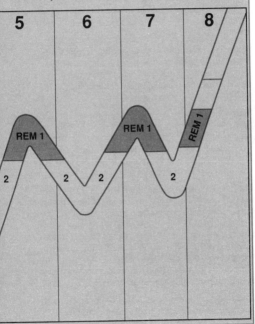

REALITY DISTORTION IN DREAMS

The world of our dreams is not bound by the rules governing the physical world. Things that are impossible in everyday life occur in dreams and do not strike the dreamer as odd in any way. Normal sense impressions can be distorted and juxtaposed in startling ways.

Time In dreams, time is of no account. Events separated by decades can be brought together into the same moment, figures from history may mingle with members of one's family, or the dreamer may be transported into a future or past time.

Space As with time, so with space – the dream world is fluid, and obeys no laws except its own. Known places, such as the office or home, can appear in far away locations, or be distorted. Your home might, for instance, acquire extra rooms, or be much larger or smaller than in real life.

Puns A woman dreaming about being a bride might be dressed in a superb white dress with a train. The sudden appearance of an electric train in the aisle of the church would seem to be very confusing, yet the link is there. Another example could be to change an isle (island) into the aisle of a church. The dream would be using two meanings of 'train' and 'isle/aisle'. Some of these puns can be private within the family, perhaps based upon familiar family names or words.

Emotion Very many dreams are accompanied by strong feelings. They are dramatic and the events and emotions tend to be exaggerated. In some strange way they appear to lack any sense of right or wrong. Some of the horrific scenes experienced in dreams seem not to be judged in the same way as if they took place in reality.

Content Familiar scenes, objects and people are often the symbols through which the unconscious communicates with the waking mind. When dreams seem to replay the past, the events or perhaps the mood are never exactly the same as in the original happening.

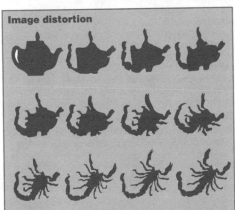

Image distortion

Dreams are not constrained by the bounds of the physical world. A teapot, for example, can become a scorpion by metamorphosis.

THE PSYCHE AND DREAMS

We need to dream and we all dream, but we don't all remember our dreams – no one knows why we forget them so easily. Throughout the ages, the questions of why we need to dream at all, and what dreams signify, have raised endless debate.

A neurophysiological explanation – which suggests that sensory signals to the brain during REM sleep trick the sleeper into believing he or she is having real experiences – does not tell us why dreams happen. Nor does it explain why dreams are so creative and richly narrative.

It has been suggested, however, that dreams are somehow connected with learning and remembering and with the integration of new experiences into the memory bank. This explains why so many dreams relate to recent events and preoccupations. They may also stand in for experiences and allow us to learn from events without having to live through them.

Psychological theories about dreams

Sigmund Freud (1856–1939) Although the idea of the unconscious has been known in Europe since the late 18th century – mainly through the writings of German philosophers – it was the Viennese psychiatrist Freud who first developed a theory about the role of the unconscious in the life of the individual.

According to Freud, the dream works on two levels. A straightforward level shows surface or 'manifest' events as remembered. In the hidden or 'latent' level, objects and actions in the dream symbolize sexual and aggressive feelings and ideas, an individual's wishes that are normally repressed. Dreams protect the sleeper from the disturbing effects of a direct realization of these wishes. The ego is driven by reality, and morality is developed in the superego to suppress the id, the childish part of the self that seeks pleasure. The dream taps into this desire for wish-fulfilment when the controlling ego is relaxed during sleep.

As Freud wrote: 'All dreams are in a sense dreams of convenience: they help to prolong sleep instead of waking up. Dreams are the guardians of sleep and not its disturbers.'

Alfred Adler (1870–1937) Another Austrian, and originally a disciple of Freud, Adler urged that the desire for power (he called it 'individual psychology') is what drives each person. Children start with a feeling of inferiority. Adults attempt to move towards goals of success and superiority, and dreams reflect these ambitions.

C.G. Jung (1875–1961) Carl Jung agreed with Freud that a dream's content uses symbolic language, but he also believed it expresses so-called collective (or archetypal) racial unconscious memories and instincts shared by all peoples, regardless of culture. These are basic ideas that are themselves symbols. They include the hero, the monster, the mother, the mandala (representing the dreamer's search for completeness and self-unity), the sacrifice and the mask.

In one reference, Jung wrote: 'It is true that there are dreams which embody suppressed wishes and fears, but what is there which the dream cannot on occasion embody? Dreams may give expression to ineluctable [inescapable] truths, to philosophical pronouncements, illusions, wild fantasies, . . . anticipations, irrational experiences, even telepathic visions, and heaven knows what besides.' They also indicate the way towards self-actualization. Jungian therapy deals extensively with dreams and fantasies.

Fritz Perls (1893–1970) The dream theory of another influential psychologist is equally fascinating. Perls, the founder of Gestalt therapy (a method of bringing alienated parts of the personality into harmony with each other), believed that the characters and objects in our dreams are projections of ourselves – parts of our personality that we do not accept or acknowledge – and of our views of others. Since we are the creators of our dreams, everything in them must be aspects of our inner selves, personal creations rather than a universal symbolic language.

Psychological theories about dreams
- Freud believed that dreams use symbols that do not disturb – they allow unconscious feeling to surface in disguise.
- Adler believed dreams reflect the individual's will for power.
- Jung believed that dreams come from the personal and also the collective unconscious.
- Perls believed that everything in our dreams is a projection of ourselves.

DREAM TOPICS

Dreams are very individual, yet they contain every conceivable thing. They rarely deal with significant national or international events or other happenings outside the immediate concerns of the dreamer. And they often seem to contain trivial objects and experiences. Among the most usual themes are: journeys, houses, water, nudity, falling, losing, finding, flying, chases, loose teeth, snakes, royalty and death. Dreams of misfortune are also universal, as are dreams of sex and aggression, of food and eating, of family and friends (present or past) and of animals.

Out-of-this-world sources

If, as some people believe, we have lived previous lives, this might explain some of the more obscure elements in our dreams. Or perhaps we dream other people's dreams for them. This might account for some nightmares that are especially difficult to interpret. It has been suggested the presence of other alien features in dreams may be the result of forces outside our time and our planet.

Universal, timeless nature of dreams

Work done by the American experimental dream researcher Calvin Hall in the 1950s and 1960s has shown that the same themes tend to occur in some people's dreams throughout their lives, despite outward changes in fortune. Dreams thus appear to have a timeless quality.

Aggression

Hall also found that dreams of aggression are common to a number of diverse cultures, including the Zulus of southeast Africa, northern Europeans, and Australian Aborigines. According to Hall, 50% of dreams contain at least one act of aggression, ranging from conciously unexpressed feelings of hostility and threats to fights and murder.

Children's dreams

Hall found that the dreams of children contain twice as much aggression as those of adults. Children also frequently dream of being attacked or chased by

Dreams for all times

A seller of dream interpretations in the 18th century

animals, wild or domesticated. These include dogs,
cats, alligators, gorillas, snakes and spiders. Perhaps in
dreams, animals dramatize a child's own wishes and
fears.

Nightmares

Research has shown that terrifying dreams tend to occur
in the second half of the night, during REM sleep. They
strike sleepers at any age, from two years old onwards,
and seem to trouble women more than men. Probably
they represent a problem that is not being confronted in
the sleeper's waking life.

According to psychiatrist Ernest Hartmann of Boston,

Books and pamphlets offering interpretations of dreams were popular in the 18th and 19th centuries. However, the interpretations they offered usually dated back to Artemidorus some 800 years ago. This example dates from the late 19th century.

THE DREAMER'S TRUE FRIEND.

1,000 DREAMS

Wherein is explained all the phenomena of spiritual imagination in Dreams, &c.

USA, those who suffer from nightmares tend to be open personalities – not only open to other people, but to their own wishes and fears. They have, he says, 'thin boundaries' in which their normal, hostile impulses are able to bypass psychological defences and invade their dreams.

Sexual dreams

These often express suppressed sexuality in an explicit way. During 'wet dreams', often experienced by adolescent males, there is involuntary emission of semen.

Incubus and succubus An incubus is a male demon who comes to sleeping women and attempts to have sexual intercourse with them. The female equivalent is a succubus. These demons were used to account for the fact that people had 'improper' dreams of which they might feel ashamed. In the 19th century, representations of this type of dream were circulated widely by pornographers hoping to take advantage of the prevailing attitude of sexual repression and prudishness.

Common dreams
- Dreams contain universal themes, from falling to animals.
- Aggression is common to all cultures and among children.
- Some people experience the same dream themes repeatedly throughout their lives.
- Nightmares may symbolize unresolved problems.
- Sexual dreams are often explicit.

Dream demons

Two pictures showing visits from the incubus. Dating from the 19th century, they show the pornographic uses to which belief in the incubus was put.

3. Types of dreams

The subjects, themes, events and objects that appear in
dreams, as well as the timing and connections, are
infinitely varied and frequently strange. It is accepted
that dreams often serve a variety of purposes in our
lives. They can alert us to problems and even
sometimes provide solutions. They release inner
tensions, give glimpses into the future and inspire the
artist. They range from residual dreams relating to daily
events, healing and safety-valve dreams to repetitive,
creative and clairvoyant dreams. Some dreams can
combine several types. Each one is unique, but they
sometimes share certain underlying features.

SAFETY-VALVE DREAMS
Freud's theory
The Austrian founder of psychoanalysis, Sigmund
Freud, whose book *The Interpretation of Dreams*
(1900) probed deep into the mysterious cosmos of
dreams, believed that dreams can reflect psychological
conflict. These are known as safety-valve dreams. They
are a means of wish-fulfilment, and they express
desires (often in a heavily disguised manner) that we
are unwilling to admit freely in waking life. These
dreams are usually brief and are the most difficult to
recognize, since we prefer not to admit hidden distress
to our conscious minds.

Freud believed that unconsciously all dreams are sexual
or aggressive, even if not apparently so. He listed
objects that symbolize sex: 'All elongated objects, such
as sticks, tree trunks and umbrellas, may stand for the

Dream types

Safety-valve
These express deep inner conflicts that are repressed at conscious level.

Clairvoyant
These warn the dreamer, or reveal anxiety concerning future events, health, or other dangers.

Creative
Subjects and themes encountered in dreams can be applied to the development of artistic activity.

Problem-solving
Solutions to problems and obstacles in daily life are often revealed in dreams.

Repetitive and sequential
Recurring dreams or repetition of themes within dreams can act as a reminder of circumstances that the dreamer has repressed in waking life.

Factual
Dreams that focus on events and circumstances from the dreamer's daily life can be influenced by sounds and other disturbances.

Compensatory
These offer satisfactions not available to the dreamer in real life. A shy individual, for example, may dream of great social success.

Physiological
Dreams may be influenced by physical discomfort or need, or sexual stirrings.

male organ, as well as long sharp weapons, such as knives, daggers and pikes . . . . Rooms in dreams are usually women.'

The phenomenon of dreams as safety-valves is illustrated in the example given below by one of Freud's most brilliant pupils, Sandor Ferenczi. Freud's concept of dreams as a safety-valve for repressed wishes is not universally accepted. Indeed, a few critics do not find any evidence that sexual and

---

A safety-valve dream

A patient dreamt that she was strangling a little white dog. The patient had told her analyst that she enjoyed cooking and often had to wring the necks of pigeons or chickens.

She also remarked that this was the manner in which she had strangled the little dog in her dream.

The dream analysed

Ferenczi asked if she had a grudge against anyone in particular. She said she disliked her sister-in-law, whom she believed was trying 'to come between my husband and myself, like a tame dove'.

Then she remembered a recent argument with her sister-in-law in which she had told her: 'Get out, I don't want a dog that bites in my house!'

The woman's real desire to strangle her sister-in-law – obviously impossible for her to do in her waking life – was accomplished harmlessly in this safety-valve dream through the use of a stand-in, the dog, according to Freudian interpretation.

aggressive drives find release in dreams or that every dream has its source in wish-fulfilment.

Safety-valve dreams
- according to Freud, allow us to behave in a way not acceptable in waking life
- symbolize wish-fulfilment and urgent desires
- may help to resolve deep, inner conflict
- may be hard to interpret because they are presented in symbols (see chapter 6)

CLAIRVOYANT DREAMS

When we dream of events or situations in the future, very often of a worrying nature, they can be ascribed to ESP, or paranormal abilities. But they could perhaps be caused by unconscious absorption of clues and repressed anxieties. Clairvoyant dreams are of two kinds: warning dreams and anxiety dreams.

Clairvoyant dreams
- show knowledge the dreamer could not have acquired through 'normal' means
- may reflect deep fears
- could be the result of 'clues' picked up during waking
- seem to suggest knowledge of the future
- frequently foretell disaster

Warning dreams

One type of prophetic, or precognitive, dream seems to act as a look into the future and, often, a warning of danger. Only sometimes is the dreamer included in the events.

Foretelling his own death, Abraham Lincoln, the 16th president of the United States, was a spectator in a dream he had about the death of the president a few days before his assassination in 1865.

But dreams of death do not always mean actual, physical death. They can mean the end of one cycle of life and the beginning of another or that the dreamer's feelings about someone have died – or that their warm feelings about the dreamer have changed.

Anxiety dreams

The mind unconsciously absorbs information that can be released in dreams. Their interpretation seems to indicate some kind of prior knowledge.

In his *Book of Dreams and Ghosts* (1897) Andrew Lang describes the case of a barrister who went out at night to post some letters. Later, despite searching anxiously, he was unable to find a cheque he had received that day. He dreamt he saw the cheque curled around a railing near his front door. When he awoke he found the cheque exactly where his dream had located it. Most probably he had subconsciously noted its fall when he went out to the postbox.

A sombre mood and the frightening content of some dreams can indicate health problems – perhaps the body is trying to provoke some action for treatment. One woman, for instance, dreamt that she saw the roof of her house pierced by the branches of a tree torn loose in a hurricane: the next day she suffered a stroke.

In the famous dream of Calpurnia, wife of the Roman emperor Julius Caesar, she dreamt that her husband was killed in the Senate. He ignored her warning and was stabbed to death the next day.

A remarkable example concerns a Norwegian fisherman named Johnson, who, just two days before the *Titanic* sank in November 1907, dreamed that a voice told him a great liner called the *Titanic* would sink after colliding with an iceberg. Johnson awoke in a sweat, then fell asleep again and returned to his dream, in which he became uneasy and felt icy waves crashing around his body.

An anxiety dream

A woman who had recently felt a lump in her breast dreamt that her husband told her that everything would be all right. In her dream, she then suddenly found herself at the seashore alone, as it got dark. The shore was empty, except for some barges.

The dream analysed

Analysis showed she had little respect for her husband's opinion. The barges reminded her of Egyptian death barges she had seen in a museum. The whole scene was deeply gloomy and the atmosphere of death was very strong. The lump in her breast was cancerous, and it was too late to stop it spreading.

CREATIVE DREAMS

Artists, writers, musicians, scientists and inventors have
acknowledged dreams as a source of original ideas and
inspiration. Remembered glimpses of a dream, its
fantasy, exaggeration, drama and emotion, have
released in them a flood of creative energy.

Music from dreams

The 18th-century Italian composer Giuseppe Tartini
called one of his pieces 'The Devil's Sonata' because
he was able to complete it only after remembering just
one trill from a dream – in which the devil had played
the violin for him.

Poetry from dreams

The poem 'Kubla Khan' was conceived by the 18th-
century English poet Samuel Taylor Coleridge while in

an opium-induced sleep. On waking, he immediately started writing, but was called away from his desk for an hour. When he returned, all that remained of his vision was a tantalizing fragment and a dim recollection of the whole poem, '. . . all the rest had passed away like the images on the surface of a stream'.

Dreams as inspiration

Charles Dickens (1812–1870) derived the inspiration for many of his characters, as well as some of his famously intricate plots, from dream material.

The Scottish author Robert Louis Stevenson also had a singularly creative dream: he dreamt that his fictional character, Hyde, 'changed personality by taking a special powder', and it was this dream-scene that formed the basis for Stevenson's great novel *The Strange Case of Dr Jekyll and Mr Hyde* (1886).

Paintings from dreams

In dreams, artists have overcome blocks or problems in their work. It was in a dream that the French artist Paul Gauguin (1848–1903) saw the vision that became his recumbent Tahitian girl in *The Spirit Watches* (1899). More deliberately, the Surrealists, as proclaimed in their manifesto (1924), aimed to 'reconcile the contradiction which has hitherto existed between dream and reality' in their work. In particular, Salvador Dalí's strange mix of ingredients captures in paint some of the fantasy of the dream world.

Creative dreams

- have inspired poetry, stories, music, painting and inventions
- are often produced by a mind relaxed after working
- can be stimulated deliberately in lucid dreaming

PROBLEM-SOLVING DREAMS

Dreams are often thought to contain the answers to problems faced in our waking lives. Many people deliberately leave decision-making to the next morning, after they've had a chance to 'dream it over'.

Some scientists and mathematicians have used dreams to help solve problems. Thomas Edison (1848–1931), American inventor, took catnaps while working and was convinced some of his best inventions came to him while dozing. The celebrated 19th-century German chemist Friedrich August Kekule von Stradovitz, for instance, dozing in front of the fire, dreamt of a snake-like arrangement of atoms. It was chasing and eating its own tail, and forming a closed chain. Kekule's dream led him to discover that the atoms of the benzene molecule are arranged in a circle, and not in a straight line, as had been thought.

The 19th-century chemist Kekule dreamed of a serpent eating its tail, which inspired him to find the molecular arrangement of the benzene molecule.

Problem-solving dreams
- can offer solutions to seemingly insoluble puzzles
- may provide guidance in decision-making

REPETITIVE AND SEQUENTIAL DREAMS

Although no two dreams are identical, some, recurring over months or even years, repeat the same content or

A repetitive dream

A man repeatedly dreamt that the lifts in the 15-storey office building where he worked were out of order, so that he had to walk down 14 flights of steep, open stairs. Terrified of falling, he would cling to the rails and somehow never reached the bottom, always waking in a sweat beforehand.

The dream analysed

Analysis revealed, eventually, a deeply rooted fear that he was not performing successfully at work and would never achieve promotion.

Sequential dreams

In the first dream the dreamer saw a man go into a dark, depressing valley, with threatening clouds. In the second dream, he was in an army mess. He wanted a table by himself, but this was refused. In the third dream he fought with and knocked out a friend, whom he thinks is arrogant.

The dreams analysed

Analysis showed that the first dream indicated that the dreamer suffered from depression. The second dream indicated the source of the depression: he is selfish, self-willed, anti-social, and unpopular. In the third dream, the friend represents himself. In knocking him out, the dreamer is trying to get rid of his own arrogance and thereby improve his situation.

important elements. The theme may be anxiety, flight from persecutors or it may involve a task that can never be properly finished; if accurately interpreted, the recurring dream may reveal the dreamer's nature. The type of dream is an attempt to recognize hidden problems, and it may hint at a solution.

Often the setting harks back to a frightening incident in childhood. A child criticized by a parent may later dream of being on trial. Rigid toilet training is said by psychoanalysts sometimes to lead to dreams of being unable to complete a particular task. Many people, even in later life, often dream of being back at school. Fear of authority may be the reason, but equally so may be a desire for the happy comradeship of those years.

Underlying causes

In many repetitive dreams, however, the original cause has not been properly dealt with but has been grafted onto another problem. Nerys Dee, in her *The Dreamer's Workbook,* tells of a woman who dreamt again and again that she was in a lion's den and was about to be attacked by one of the animals. This repetitive dream shows that the dreamer has reached an impasse and cannot find a way out of a problem.

Repetitive and sequential dreams
- may occur on one night, over several nights, or over years
- if frightening, may be due to anxieties from childhood

FACTUAL DREAMS

As well as being symbolic, dreams can also be factual and logical. These dreams are usually about everyday objects and characters known to the dreamer. Fairly easy to understand, they deal with daily, often trivial experiences.

One dream, recounted in Nerys Dee's *The Dreamer's Workbook*, was set in a department store. The dreamer stole a lipstick from the cosmetic counter and put it into a large holdall. But before she walked out, a store detective came up and arrested her. After waking, she remembered painfully something that had happened the previous year. This dream was clearly acting as a warning against any further shoplifting by reactivating the bad feelings brought about by the dreamer's public arrest.

Vigilant dreams are factual dreams that incorporate elements of the surroundings of the sleeper into the dream: a dripping tap, passing traffic, a ticking clock. Dreams can also serve as reminders of things we need to do. Usually simple and practical, these dreams are often quite explicit, rather than symbolic, and serve to jog the memory.

Factual dreams
- may be the means by which we absorb daily happenings
- can finish off the day's affairs
- may help us to resolve past difficult experiences
- sometimes include environmental noise
- do not usually have much symbolic significance

Examples of factual dreams

In one factual dream, a young man saw himself in his blue car, driving along a motorway. When he turned off on to a side road, he encountered a sudden, sharp bend and applied his brakes. These failed to work and the car hit a wall.

For the dreamer, this was a factual warning dream, provoking him into taking appropriate action, i.e. checking his brakes.

In *Dream Power*, psychologist Ann Faraday relates how she dreamt that the door to the garden was open and banging in the wind. When she awoke, she actually heard banging, though when she went downstairs to check the door, she found it was securely fixed open.

She believed that her mind had created the noise of the swinging door in order to wake her up and get her to check that the door had been properly locked.

COMPENSATORY DREAMS

The great Swiss psychoanalyst Carl Jung believed that dreams had a compensatory function – providing a psychic balance for the personality. A timid man, unable to make advances to women, may, for example, dream of having a harem. And kind individuals may dream of perpetrating great violence.

One type of compensatory dream, called a contrary dream, are temporary and give balance to a personality overwhelmed by, say, sadness, happiness or excitement. For example, during a period of grief dreams may be almost comic. At a time of personal triumph, dreams of uncontrollable grief may occur.

A compensatory dream

Jung once described a compensatory dream he
himself had, at the time when he was a devoted
disciple of Freud. Jung dreamt of Freud as a
'peevish official of the Imperial Austrian monarchy,
as a defunct and still walking ghost of a customs
inspector'.

The dream analysed

Jung interpreted his dream as compensation for– or
an antidote to – his high admiration for Freud,
knowing that he should be more critical and
cautious of his mentor's views.

Compensatory dreams
- often have content that is surprising to the
  dreamer
- may show the dreamer in a new and strange light
- help to counterbalance failings and needs
- can be a temporary reaction to extreme moods

PHYSIOLOGICAL DREAMS

The momentary or even longer-term needs and the
condition of the sleeping body may slip into dreaming,
as in sexual dreams and dreams of feeling cold or
thirsty. In one example, a man dreamt that he was being
strangled, and awoke to find he had somehow wound
the bedclothes around his neck. Women can become
aware in their dreams of being pregnant very early on.

Physiological dreams
- are directly related to the physical needs of the body
- may wake up the dreamer

A physical sensation, such as falling out of bed, can be incorporated into a dream.

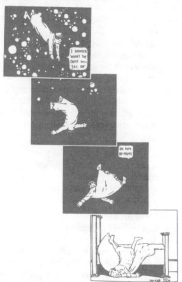

4. Lucid dreams

One of the strangest – and for many the most exhilarating – type of dream is the 'lucid' dream. In it, the dreamer becomes fully conscious, while asleep, that he or she is dreaming.

No accurate figures exist for the number of people who dream lucidly. It is generally believed that lucid dreaming is rare, but with perseverance it is a skill that can be learned.

First-time lucid dreamers often note a pleasurable heightening of the senses, especially vision, and a greater awareness of detail and surroundings; they also note that the mind shows the same consciousness as when awake. When they have learned to control events, they can indulge in wish-fulfilment and problem-solving and can learn to cope with anxieties. The sense of satisfaction and achievement remains long after they have woken up.

WHEN LUCID DREAMS OCCUR

Lucid dreams are said to be most frequent in the early morning. People suddenly realize they are dreaming because of some bizarre occurrence or striking inconsistency in the dream.

Incubating lucid dreams

People can prompt lucid dreaming in themselves. In order to dream lucidly about a particular topic or theme, you have to prepare yourself mentally by learning and practising 'dream incubation'. This takes time and perseverance. The aim is to take your consciousness

The path to lucid dreaming

1 Create a comfortable sleeping environment.
2 Have pencil and paper ready to record your dream.
3 Decide the theme or subject of your dream.
4 Think about the theme carefully during the day.
5 Describe briefly, such as 'I need to come to terms with my nightmare', 'I want to go to Paris', 'I need to decide on . . .', 'I must discuss my finances with an expert', or 'I want to fly'.
6 If you have a problem to solve, write down the facts.
7 Prepare your body for sleep (see pp. 67–68).
8 Read through your notes.
9 Go to bed immediately and think about the theme.
10 Do not think about anything else.

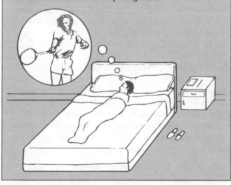

with you into the dream – or, at least, to trigger the
conscious mind while asleep.

Make sure that you are able to remember and write up
your nightly dreams. (See also chapter 5, 'Sweet
dreams'.) But don't try to control all your dreams. Give
yourself plenty of time for 'free dreaming', allowing
your unconscious to prompt in its own way your
rational mind. And it is important to try to bring up to
your consciousness any inner conflicts that are
expressed in your dreams. Only if you are prepared to
deal with these, will you avoid putting extra stress on
yourself.

TYPES OF LUCID DREAMS
Experimentation dreams
A Dutch physician, Frederick van Eeden, vividly
described the particular flavour of one lucid dream in
which he dreamt that he stood by a window at a table
on which were breakable objects. He knew he was
dreaming and decided to try some experiments. He
tried to break a glass with a stone, then with his fist,
while realizing how dangerous this would be in waking
life. The glass remained whole. Later in the dream he
looked at it again and it was broken – almost as if this
dream world were a clever fake with just a few small
failures. He threw the broken glass out of the window,
and it was snatched up by two dogs quite naturally, as if
in a comedy. He then sipped some claret from another
glass and, although he was dreaming, he noted clearly
that it had the taste of wine.

Strange and common place dreams
One woman dreamt her sister was showing her a vase

when it fell and smashed into pieces. But almost immediately the vase became whole again. The dreamer realized something was not right, and knew she must be dreaming. Similarly a man dreamt he was out walking his Jack Russell terrier in his neighbourhood. As they passed a familiar cafe, the dog startled the man by demanding an omelette and chips, so making him realize he was dreaming.

USES OF LUCID DREAMS

Control of images

The ability to direct your lucid dreaming means that you can command the characters, change the scenery or restructure the plot. You can also choose the subject. It is claimed that through dream direction, and after practice, dreamers can learn to satisfy their unconscious desires – some may date back to childhood – and banish terrors. They can solve problems, travel to exotic places, take part in historical events, meet a hero, or improve their health.

Learning through lucid dreams

Used properly, lucid dreams can reveal inner anxieties and help the emotional balance of the dreamer. Perhaps they can even tap the resources of the unconscious mind, to increase creativity.

However, the greatest benefit from lucid dreams may come from the dreamer being able to take control of his or her reactions to dream situations, usually frightening events. For example, by literally looking threatening figures in the eye, the dreamer may be able to deprive them of their ability to terrify.

Lucid dreams
- mean the dreamer is aware, because of some strange event, that he or she is dreaming
- can be directed
- come with learning
- enable wish-fulfilment, problem-solving and coping with fears

LUCID NIGHTMARES

Some people become fully lucid in nightmares. This may allow them to work through the experience, but it takes courage. Even though the most terrifying of creatures in a dream are mere phantoms, escape seems the only option. But running away does not resolve the conflict that produced the horrors.

Making peace with fear

It is not always possible, however, to make frightening dream images disappear. Hostile figures in our dreams represent sides of our psyche we want to deny. We might therefore harm ourselves by trying to annihilate them. Better to try to integrate them by making peace with them.

Lucid nightmares
- may be horrific, but confronting them may resolve the problem
- can be beneficial if peace is made within the dream

OUT-OF-BODY EXPERIENCES

Similar to lucid dreams are out-of-body experiences
(OBEs). About 10% of the population report having
had an out-of-body experience. OBEs usually last only
moments, during which consciousness seems to leave
the body and the physical self can be seen from outside.
Most commonly OBEs occur during sleep,
unconsciousness or while under anaesthesia.

One kind of OBE is the near-death experience (NDE),
which some patients have during surgery or serious
illness. Patients believe they have left the body and
entered a more serene state but are then called back to
their body because it is not yet time to die.

Some people enter the OBE state at will, either by
means of meditation or with the aid of flotation tanks.

5. Sweet dreams

In order to dream well, the body and mind need to be properly relaxed. Here we suggest things you should and should not do to encourage a good night's sleep and creative dreaming.

HOW MANY HOURS OF SLEEP ARE NEEDED?

You should work out yourself how long you need to sleep each night and, depending when you have to wake up, at what time it is best to go to bed. The amount of sleep people need varies hugely – 65% of adults need between 6.5 and 8.5 hours per night. Some can do with 5 hours, but a small minority needs as much as 10 hours each night. It is best to be in bed about half an hour before you actually need to go to sleep.

EFFECTS OF FOOD AND DRUGS

Food

What you eat, and when, often affect your pattern of sleeping and dreaming. Nightmares are sometimes blamed on heavy, late-night meals. If your digestion is troubled while you sleep, your dreams will probably reflect this problem, giving you strange and alarming visions. Before you go to bed, avoid foods that cause wind, such as beans, raw vegetables and peanuts, and other high-fat foods, like pastries or potato chips. If you must eat later than two hours before you go to bed, make it something light – like fruit and a warm, milky drink. Try to eat your main evening meal earlier, so that by the time you go to bed, the digestive process will be well under way.

Drugs

Research has shown that drinks with a high caffeine content (especially coffee but also tea) definitely prolong the time it takes to fall asleep. Some diet pills also contain stimulants, and certain medical drugs, such as tranquilizers, can affect your quality of sleep. Sleeping tablets should not be taken if you want to dream; the sleep they offer tends to be blank and dreamless. Alcohol should also be avoided late at night (and in any great quantity over a long period of time), as well as cigarettes. They suppress both the REM (dreaming) stage sleep and deep sleep, and speed up the fluctuations between them. Then, when alcohol wears off, the REM stage intrudes on other stages of your sleep, depriving the body of deep rest.

SETTING THE ENVIRONMENT

Since light is the natural cue for waking, some people can sleep only in total darkness. The bedroom should be well aired and neither too hot nor too cold.

Noise

Background noises can be seriously disturbing for sleepers, or those trying to get to sleep. Ear plugs – of the wax or sponge varieties – can muffle sounds and at least give some psychological comfort. Or you could try masking the noise with the constant sound of a fan or air conditioner. Some find a tape recording of surf or a waterfall helpful.

Comfort in bed

Do not forget the condition of the bed. It is crucial that your body should get the best possible support as you sleep. Ideally, your spine should maintain the same contours as when you are standing upright – with chin, stomach and pelvis tucked in. The mattress should be firm, but not rock hard. Some believe that the position of the bed also has an effect on sleep. Charles Dickens aligned his bed along the north–south axis so that he could benefit from the flow of magnetic currents.

Reducing tension

Before going to bed, you might find it helpful to lessen tension knots with a few exercises, such as stretching your muscles. Take a warm bath, listen to some quiet music or watch a relaxing television show. (Do not watch the TV news programmes, with their diet of disasters and sensationalism.)

Reading in bed

To relax and fall asleep quickly, try not to think about the issues of the day. Instead, perhaps read a novel or other book, one that is guaranteed to calm the mind. Some people fall asleep after reading a single page – perhaps the greatest benefit a boring book can bring!

Courting sleep

Finally, once you are in bed, if you cannot sleep, there are a number of other strategies you could try to help you drift off to slumberland. Count backwards from 1000, try to remember a poem you learned at school, or list all the boys' and girls' names you can think of in alphabetical order. Or, and this is hard, try to empty your mind completely of all thought. A physical exercise might also help. For example, tense the muscles of your toes, hold for several seconds and then relax. Then tense and relax your feet and lower legs,

moving gradually up your body to your head. Now
work downwards, back to your toes.

INSOMNIA
If you have trouble getting off to sleep, try not to go to
bed too early. Experiment with ways to relax – perhaps
you could take more exercise during the day. Some
people need a long time to fall asleep at night, wake up
very early or suffer from insomnia because they have
rested during the day.

Remedies
The answer is not to take a catnap in the
afternoon. Sleeping during the day can seriously
interfere with your sleeping pattern. Generally, it is
unwise to make a habit of daytime sleeping. If you are
an insomniac, it is better to take a few 10-minute breaks
for relaxation exercises or meditation during the day.

To sleep well and dream creatively
- work out how much sleep you need and stick to it
- be careful of what you eat and drink late in the day
- avoid caffeine, nicotine, alcohol and pills before
  bed
- ensure your room is dark, quiet, warm but not
  stuffy
- check that your bed is as comfortable as it can be
- exercise lightly to relieve tension and have a bath
- choose a relaxing read to end the day

To help insomnia
- Avoid catnapping during the day, try to take more
  exercise or practise meditation

---

6. Symbolism

Most of our dreams have a very important symbolic
content, for dreams are the way the subconscious
speaks to us. It sometimes does so in terms of puns or
plays on words. For example, to dream of a mirror may
refer to a feeling that things are reversed or not quite
right in your life, a fear that you are not presenting your
true self to the world, or a realization that at long last
you need to face up to things. Likewise, a dream of a
game of chess may symbolize a battle or struggle, a
desire for intellectual stimulation, or even a suppressed
desire for a 'mate'.

This chapter is devoted to the language of dreams and
the interpretations of dream activities. Consult it
whenever you are intrigued by the subject matter of a
dream. Remember, however, that dreams are by their
nature unique and individual, so that any guide to
interpretation can never be definitive. Rather, use it to
help you consider more deeply the likely significance
of certain dream elements so that you may draw your
own conclusions and thereby gain greater
understanding of yourself.

Classification of content

Meanings have been classified throughout with the aid
of symbols, so that you can see at a glance whether a
category of dream holds good, bad or mixed news.

✖ = good
● = longing or desire
✚ = warning
◆ = bad

Abandonment

◆ **Being abandoned** – if by a friend or relative, there will be illness around you.

✖ **Abandoning bad elements** – you will gain financially.

◆ ● **Abandoning close family** – a sign of trouble, unless dreamt by a young person about to leave home, when it presages forthcoming independence.

✖ **Witness to an abandonment** – you will soon receive some important news.

Abattoir

◆ ✚ This is likely to be a warning of some impending disaster.

See also **Butcher**

Abduction

● **Abducting someone** – power is what you desire.

◆ **Being abducted** – you are fearful of conflict at the present time. You probably fear leaving the family circle, or that you will one day be left alone and have to be entirely self-sufficient. This sort of dream has also been known to occur to a newly engaged woman who has just been introduced to her in-laws and who feels they are somehow trying to influence her.

See also **Bandits, Rape**

Abnormality

✖ To see objects with strange elements means a good outcome to a worrying situation.

Abortion

◆ **Dreamt by a man** – the chances are that the dreamer feels guilty about some aspect of life, not necessarily connected with fatherhood.

✚ **Dreamt by a woman** – a form of warning dream, reflects anxiety about an activity that you are about to embark upon.
See also **Baby**

Abroad
● You desire to escape your present environment.
✖ This may also be predictive of making new friends and changing one's lifestyle.
See also **Travel**

Abuse
✚ ◆ **Abused by someone else** – you will have an illness.
✖ **Abusing someone else** – you can probably expect some financial improvement.

Abyss
◆ **Falling into an abyss** – a sign of fear of disappointment in life, or that you will fail to face up to a series of problems.
✖ **Peering into an abyss** – a sign that you will be able to cope with any burdens that arise.
See also **Cliff, Falling**

Accelerator
✖ **Pressing car accelerator** – by continuing your efforts you will reach your goal.
✚ **Being unable to decelerate** – a warning to stop bad behaviour.

Accent
✖ **Speaking with a foreign accent** – indicative of forthcoming travel.

✘ **Hearing someone else speaking with an accent** –
you will soon make an important new acquaintance
who will play a major role in your life.
See also **Language, Travel**

Accident
♦ **At sea** – relates to fears about a possible break-up of
a long-standing relationship.
✚ **Car crash** – take special care when driving or even
as a pedestrian for the next few days, in case the dream
is predictive.
♦ **In the home** – reflects an anxiety about
relationships within the family circle.
♦ **Plane crash** – business worries and financial
concerns are indicated.
See also **Falling**

Accordion
✘ **Playing one** – indicates a happy and lasting love
affair will come your way, though you may experience
some sadness in achieving it.
♦ **Hearing one** – indicates that some sadness will
enter your life.

Accounts
✚ **Argument with your accountant or the tax
inspector** – a self-generated warning to remain in the
black and not spend beyond your means.
✘ **Balancing the books** – predictive of a windfall.
See also **Money**

Accusation
♦ **Accused by someone else** – you probably have a
guilty secret.

◆ **Accusing someone else** – you may very soon have to face up to having been taken for a ride by someone unscrupulous.
See also **Judge**

Ace

✘ **Of hearts** – denotes success in love.

✘ **Of diamonds** – means financial good fortune.

◆ **Of spades** – predicts work unrewarded.

◆ **Of clubs** – you may soon suffer disgrace.

Ache

✚ **Headache** – you should not tell anyone of your work plans.

✘ **In the abdomen** – you will enjoy good health.

✘ **In the arms or legs** – you can expect to be content with life.

Acid

◆ **Drinking acid** – indicates great anxiety concerning your debts.

◆ **Seeing acids** – you may discover someone scheming against you.

Acorns

✘ **Seeing acorns on the ground** – you will enjoy good fortune.

✘ **Picking acorns up** – presages a successful outcome to your labours.

✚ **Picking unripe acorns from a tree** – warns against too much haste in carrying out your plans.

Acrobatics

◆ **Watching an acrobat** – a sign that you are feeling inadequate in daily life.

⌘ **Performing acrobatics yourself** – a sign that you will be able to overcome current problems and escape potential danger.

Actor/actress

♦ **Poor performance** – you lack the confidence to face up to some imminent event.
⌘ **Starring role** – predictive of forthcoming success at work.
See also **Applause, Theatre**

Adam and Eve

● **Meeting the first man and woman** – desire for universal harmony and peace.
♦ **Self as Adam or Eve** – undue concern about an intimate relationship.

Admiration

⌘ ✚ **Being admired by others** – indicates self-confidence but may be warning you of forthcoming illness.
⌘ **Admiring others** – you are heading towards prosperity.

Adoption

● **Adopting a child** – you not only long to take on the parental role but need to find an outlet for all that love and affection you have been storing up.
♦ **Adopted as a child** – could be a sign of instability within the family circle and a desire to find relations with whom you might be more compatible.
See also **Child/children, Family, Parents**

Adultery

♦ ● **Committed by self** – simple wish-fulfilment, or

you are harbouring guilty feelings. A woman dreaming that she is someone's mistress may be suffering anxiety about her financial security.

◆ **Committed by spouse** – reflects a constant nagging concern over possible infidelity.

✖ **Resisted** – a sign that you will overcome current difficulties in life by sheer resolve.

See also **Divorce, Infidelity, Marriage**

Advancement
✖ Straightforwardly, a sign of improved circumstances.

Adventure
✖ **Enjoyable experience** – you can look forward to forthcoming good news.

◆ **Terrifying experience** – you fear breaking free from a restrictive set routine.

Aeroplane *See* **Accident, Flying, Journeys, Travel**

Affliction
✖ Strangely, to dream of physical affliction generally means good health.

Aggression
◆ **A woman's dream of an aggressive man** – reflects fear of a sexual assault.

◆ **Aggressive female in man or woman's dream** – represents fear of the mother figure.

◆ **A man's dream of an aggressive man** – indicates fear of being beaten in the promotion stakes at work, or even of losing one's job.

See also **Fight, Quarrel, Rape**

Alcohol

✖ **Drink in moderation** – a sign of future success and happiness.

◆ ✦ **Drinking to excess** – fear of being discovered for what one really is. It can also be a warning from the subconscious about the dangers of excess in other areas of life.
See also **Drink, Drunkenness, Wine**

Aliens

◆ Extraterrestrials in dreams point to anxiety over personal safety – either physically or financially.
See also **Rocket**

Alley

◆ **With a dead-end** – you are concerned about what seems to be some inescapable situation.

✖ **With a way-out** – you are aware deep down that, with considerable effort, a current problem could soon be put behind you.
See also **Road**

Altar *See* **Church, Sacrifice**

Altitude

✦ If you look down from a great height, this means you may be about to make a great mistake.

Ambulance

◆ **Seeing an ambulance** – you may be feeling anxious about behaving indiscreetly.

◆ **Being carried in one** – expresses a fear that you will experience an emergency.

◆ **Someone else carried in one** – an expression of hostility and perhaps wish-fulfilment.

Ambush
✛ **Being ambushed yourself** – warns against difficulties at work or at home.

✖ **Staging an ambush** – you may be pleasantly surprised by the outcome of some impending event.

Amethyst
✖ **Seeing an amethyst** – expresses contentment with life.

◆ **Losing an amethyst** – indicates a worry about losing a friend through illness or a quarrel.

Ammunition
✖ Dreams about ammunition point to successfully completed work.

◆ **Depleted or lost ammunition** – you may feel you are involved in pointless struggles, or a quarrel may be brewing with your partner.

Amputation
◆ **Losing a limb** – difficulties lie ahead.

◆ **Another's amputation** – you are probably feeling guilty about not devoting enough time, patience or financial resources to someone else.
See also **Doctor, Hospital, Surgeon**

Amusement park
✖ **Enjoying the rides** – a sign of forthcoming good fortune.

◆ **Frightening experience** – it could be that you are suspicious of the underlying motives of others and fear that you will finally lose out.
See also **Circus, Fairground, Falling, Merry-go-round**

Ancestors

● ◆ This dream is often a plea for help.
See also **Family, Grandparents**

Anchor

✚ A sign that some current relationship requires a rather firmer basis.
See also **Boat, Ship, Shipwreck**

Angels

◆ ✖ Predictively, this is a sign of forthcoming peace and prosperity. But, sometimes, such a dream is indicative of concern over judgment for one's conduct on earth.
See also **Death, God, Heaven**

Anima/animus *See* **Glossary**

Animals

✖ ◆ **Antelopes** – if you see antelopes you may anticipate financial gain; if you shoot one, you are fearing persecution.

◆ **Apes** – you are worried that others are taking advantage of your good nature.

● **Baby animals** – newborn creatures in dreams point to a desire to procreate.

◆ ✖ **Cats** – consider your attitude to cats in everyday life and you should find a clue to their symbolism in your particular dream, since they may either represent cunning or pure contentment. Seeing a kitten means the dreamer's affections are being played with. Playing with a kitten means you will suffer many small irritations.

◆ ● **Cows** – such a dream either is symbolic of a

desire to raise a family or could reflect a fear of being seen as stupid.

♦ ✖ ● **Dogs** – the first thing you must do is decide whether the dog represents yourself or someone else. Then examine its behaviour in the dream. Are you perhaps seeking a friend? Have you been as loyal as you could have been of late? Dreaming of being bitten by a lap dog may reveal a hidden concern about trouble with a jealous partner or spouse, or anxiety about a subordinate at work scheming against you.

✚ **Gnu** – Your subconscious is trying to tell you to get out of doors more and get some novelty into your life.

♦ ✖ **Horses** – if you dream of being taken for a ride, that may be precisely how you feel deep-down. On the other hand, a dream of horses can signify guilt over riding over others. Riding a horse can also represent the sexual act in a dream. Dreaming of a horse's mane, regardless of its colour, is an omen of unexpected irritation.

♦ **Lions and other wild animals** – generally signify fear of one's own emotions.

♦ **Snakes** – reflect sexual fears but also indicative of anxiety over deviousness or some malign force.
See also **Birds, Insects, Zoo**

Anniversary
✖ All anniversaries, birthdays, weddings etc. mean happy family meetings.

Antelopes *See* Animals

Antiques *See* Furniture

Ants *See* Insects

Anxiety
● ◆ May relate to present worries. It might be about differences between the way the dreamer would like to live and how he or she actually lives.

Apparitions *See* **Ghosts**

Apes *See* **Animals**

Applause
◆ ● This is a sign that you seek recognition for efforts previously unrewarded. Alternatively, you may inwardly fear that while others offer praise, deep down they are envious of you.
See also **Actor/Actress, Theatre**

Appointments
◆ ✚ **Missing an appointment** – you may be worried about missing an opportunity, or feel concerned that you are failing in some duty.

Argument
◆ **A quarrel** can be a sign that a relationship is getting stale and needs some other element to it.
◆ **If you lose your temper** – you may make decisions too quickly.
✖ **If you don't lose your temper** – luck will come your way.

Army
◆ You have many difficulties to overcome in order to achieve your ultimate ambitions.
See also **Fight, Soldiers**

Arrival *See* **Journeys**

Arrow

● ♦ **Shooting an arrow at someone** – depending on its context – may express a wish to have a sexual relation with someone or a wish to kill or injure them.

♦ **Missing a target** – you are experiencing difficulties in your efforts to communicate with someone.

♦ ✚ **Being struck by an arrow** – warns you against situations in which you may be disgraced.

Artist

♦ **Watching an artist at work** – you are aware, even if unconsciously, that you are wasting a good deal of time right now, rather than taking practical steps to resolve a situation.

● **Self as an artist** – you yearn for public recognition and an opportunity to demonstrate creative prowess.
See also **Painting**

Ashes

♦ You may be afraid of death, or perhaps you don't admit that basically you feel insignificant.

Assault *See* **Aggression, Attack, Fight**

Asthma *See* **Illness**

Astrologer

● You are probably seeking an excuse for making dramatic changes in your life.

Astronomer *See* **Scientist**

Asylum

♦ This dream is a pointer to deep concerns regarding personal well-being and safety.
See also **Hospital**

Attack

♦ **Being attacked** – you probably feel very vulnerable on an emotional level.

♦ **Attacking someone** – a sign of deep resentment or that there is some action you would like to take in waking life but which you fear because the result is uncertain.

See also **Abduction, Aggression, Fight, Rape**

Audience *See* **Actor/Actress, Applause, Theatre**

Avalanche

✚ ✖ A warning of some terrifying experience to come – one, however, that you will survive and from which you will almost certainly benefit.

See also **Accident**

Award

● ✖ You are probably going through a lucky patch right now or secretly hanker after greater recognition for efforts at work.

See also **Applause, Prize, Royalty**

Baby

♦ **Crying babies** – usually significant of poor health.

✖ **Bonny, smiling baby** – denotes feelings of security and happiness.

♦ **Bathing a baby and letting it disappear down the plug-hole** – points to fears of not living up to what is expected of one.

♦ **Ugly baby** – you fear someone else's motives.

See also **Abortion, Child/children, Family**

Baby animals *See* **Animals**

Bachelor
● **Happy bachelor** – if a man dreams of being a happy-go-lucky bachelor when, in waking life, he is married, the probability is that he hankers after his former single existence.

◆ **Elderly bachelor** – you fear loss of your spouse and of being left alone.
See also **Marriage**

Baker/baking
✖ Such dreams are generally indicative of forthcoming success and a 'rise' in salary or status.

Baldness
◆ **Dreamt by a man** – points to fear of loss of financial security.

◆ **Dreamt by a woman** – a sure sign that she is concerned about her health and also loss of sex appeal.
See also **Barber, Hair**

Ball games *See* **Games**

Balloon
● **Playing with a balloon** – since the shape of balloons is reminiscent of breasts, this dream may indicate a wish for a sexual encounter; it may also recall happy childhood experiences.

● **In flight** – reflects a desire to rise above life's problems and escape to some fantasy world.

◆ **Descending** – a prophecy of some form of setback to your plans.
See also **Flying**

Bandits
◆ **The dreamer is attacked** – you fear, unconsciously, that you are being taken advantage of in everyday life.
◆ **The dreamer as the bandit** – this is a reflection of deep-rooted guilt over some former action.
See also **Abduction, Burglary, Crime, Robbery**

Bank
◆ You are probably fearful of some forthcoming confrontation – whether at home or in a work situation. But if the bank manager is unexpectedly amiable, more than likely you are aware that you are worrying over nothing.
See also **Bankruptcy, Money, Robbery**

Bankruptcy
◆ This is a sure sign of incipient depression and despair, even if in waking life there may be no pressing financial problems. Quite possibly, you know deep down that you have not taken heed of lessons offered by past experiences.

Banquet
◆ This could well reflect an inner awareness that you are over-concerned with trivialities and have neglected more basic and important factors.
See also **Eating, Food, Party**

Barber
◆ You fear loss of stamina or are anxious about some future operation or medical treatment.
See also **Baldness, Hair**

Barefoot *See* **Feet**

Bargain

⌘ You will succeed at a project. If a woman sees a bargain sale, the outlook is good.

Bath

♦ **Taking a bath** – you may be harbouring some real or imagined guilt you wish to be rid of.
♦ **Someone else bathing** – indicates a feeling that someone has wronged you.

Battle

♦ ✚ Taking part in a confrontation between two armies in a dream may reflect some battle in which you are engaged in waking life, whether at home, at work or socially. It may also be a warning that you should be prepared for some threatening event.
See also **Aggression, Army, Fight, Soldiers, War**

Beach

● **Lying on some sun-drenched beach** – probably a wish-fulfilment dream.
♦ **Working on a beach** – you fear ruin while others around you bask in financial success.
See also **Sand, Sea, Sun**

Beating

♦ **Being beaten** – probably means family rows.
✚ **Beating a child** – a warning against taking advantage of someone, especially a young person.

Beauty

⌘ ● **A beautiful woman** – predicts happiness and success in business; if dreamt by a man it may be simple wish-fulfilment.
⌘ **A beautiful child** – predicts a happy love life.

Bed *See* **Furniture**

Beggar

✖ ◆ If you help, this is a lucky sign. If you refuse help, you are in trouble.
See also **Pauper, Poverty**

Beheading

◆ **Being beheaded** – you may be worried about spending too much time on your career while ignoring personal relationships.

Bells

◆ ✖ You are probably fearful that they toll for you. Alternatively, it may be an attempt by your subconscious to remind you of something important, or a sign that you are looking forward to some form of family celebration.

Bereavement

◆ This is likely to be an indication that you feel that those around you are not as affectionate as they might be. You may also fear loneliness.
See also **Death, Funeral**

Bicycle *See* **Journeys**

Birds

◆ **Caged birds** – indicate a fear of being confined within a relationship.

◆ **Cockerel** – fighting cockerels are often a reflection of family disagreements.

● **Dove** – this worldwide symbol of peace and spiritual satisfaction indicates a striving for precisely these ideals.

● ◆ **Eagle** – a soaring eagle often reflects a concern with matters spiritual. It may also, however, point to a fear that someone ruthless is exploiting you.

● **Flocks of birds** – birds in flight signify a desire to escape some present situation and also to an intense idealism.

● ◆ **Hen** – a clear maternal symbol when encountered in a dream. A black hen, however, is predictive of bad news.

◆ **Ostrich** – may be a sign that you feel restricted or perhaps that you have been burying your head in the sand.

● ◆ **Owl** – this bird may well represent the need for the advice of someone older or wiser than yourself. Alternatively, it is sometimes seen as a symbol of death.

● **Peacock** – represents a desire for more colour and flamboyance in one's life.

● **Stork** – you may be expressing a desire for parenthood.

● **Swan** – this elegant bird is associated with beauty and fertility, for both of which the dreamer may be hankering.

See also **Cage, Nests**

Birth

◆ ● ✖ **Dreamt by a woman** – if there is no sign of pregnancy in waking life, almost certainly this is either a form of wish-fulfilment or an expression of deep-set fear, following an affair. Interpretation must depend on your feelings within the dream.

● ◆ **Dreamt by a man** – an indication that you are currently facing what seems to be an impossible task but are determined to overcome it.
See also **Baby, Child/children**

Birthday
✖ ● Considered a sign that good luck will be forthcoming. It may also reflect a desire for greater attention.
See also **Party**

Blackboard
◆ **Written on in white chalk** – predicts that bad news is on its way to you.

Blame
✖ **Being blamed** – you will have luck at work.
◆ **Blaming someone else** – you will be discontented.
✚ **Seeing someone being blamed** – watch out for hypocrisy in your circle.

Blood
◆ **Seeing blood in your dream (either your own or someone else's)** it is likely that you fear loss of strength and possibly hostility on the part of a colleague.
See also **Amputation, Doctor, Hospital, Operation, Surgeon**

Boasting
◆ ✚ Boasting in dreams may express regret for some impulsive action, or warn against using unfair means against competitors.

Boat *See* **Anchor, Journeys, Sea, Ship, Yacht**

Bomb
◆ Clearly symbolic of fear of something currently threatening your otherwise peaceful existence.
See also **War**

Bones *See* **Skeleton/skull**

Book
⌘ If you study, this means happiness and riches. Children and books mean good behaviour in young people.
See also **Illiteracy, Library, Reading**

Bookcase *See* **Furniture**

Boomerang
● **Refusing to come back** – symbolic of a need for change.
⌘ **Coming back** – generally taken as a sign of satisfaction with life.

Borrowing
◆ **Borrowing from a friend** – a sign that you are concerned about finances.
◆ **Lending to a friend** – it is likely you are used to playing the role of provider and possibly resent being relied upon for this.
See also **Bank, Money**

Bouquet *See* **Flowers**

Boy
● This can be either the dreamer when young, if

dreamt by a man, or a symbol of the dreamer's
potential, if dreamt by a man or woman.

Bravery
✖ A sign you will have the chance to show bravery, if
you have been courageous in a dream.

Bread *See* **Baker/baking**

Bride
● **Self as the bride** – probably how you would like to
see yourself in the future.
◆ **Someone else as a bride** – a sign of fear of the loss
of a friend or sister as a result of her marriage.
See also **Marriage, Wedding**

Bridegroom
◆ **Dreamt by a man** – you are usually anxious about
the prospect of marriage and losing your freedom.
See also **Marriage, Wedding**

Bridge
◆ ✖ ● **Crossing a bridge** – indicates that a transition
in your life is under way or that you want or fear one.
✚ **A broken or rickety bridge** – a warning of
disappointments to come.

Bronze
✖ **Bronze statue** – a sign that you will marry the
partner of your choice.

Brother *See* **Family, Siblings**

Bucket
◆ ● **Filling a bucket** – a sexual dream; it may express
longing or an anxiety to do with sex.

♦ **Stumbling over a bucket** – an omen of an impending death.
See also **Crime, Robbery**

Bugs *See* **Insects**

Burglary
♦ A reflection of fear of either the loss of something you value greatly or of an invasion of privacy.
See also **Crime, Robbery**

Buried alive
♦ You are making a bad mistake. If you manage to escape, your subconscious blames you for doing something morally wrong.
See also **Death, Funeral**

Burns
✖ A sign of approval from friends (burnt hands) or that you will succeed in something (feet).

Bus
✖ **Driving a bus** – you may be heading towards your goal or away from something.
♦ **Being a passenger in a bus** – expresses a worry that someone else is controlling your life.
♦ **Missing a bus** – you may be fearful of missing out on something you want.
♦ **Being on a stationary bus** – indicates that you feel trapped in a situation with which you are unhappy.

Butcher
♦ **Someone else as a butcher** – indicates a fear that someone is out to destroy your happiness for personal benefit.

◆ **Being a butcher yourself** – you may be revealing extremely aggressive and hostile feelings.

Butterflies *See* **Insects**

Cage

◆ You are unable to rid yourself of inhibitions and you feel restricted by the confines of family life.

● **Freeing a bird from a cage** – traditionally, a symbol of lost virginity.

See also **Birds, Zoo**

Caged birds *See* **Birds**

Candles

● **Lit** – you are unconsciously seeking comfort and spiritual warmth.

◆ **Unlit** – you fear rejection.

◆ **A candle burning to nothing** – may express fears of death or longing for release; for men, it reflects worry about waning sexual powers.

Cannibals

◆ **Being eaten** – symbolic of the evil motives that you suspect are harboured by others.

◆ **Dreamer as the cannibal** – you have a long-held resentment that has not yet found an outlet.

Car *See* **Accident, Journeys**

Cart

◆ **Riding in a cart** – misfortune will come your way.

✖ **Driving a cart** – you will achieve success in business matters.

✖ **Lovers together in a cart** – indicates fidelity and a happy partnership.

Castles

✄ **Living in a castle** – you feel safe from enemies and rivals.

● **Seeing a castle** – you may be longing for greater security or wishing to escape from something in your life.

Castration

◆ **Dreamt by a man** – this is no doubt a reflection of deepest fears of loss of status and manhood.

◆ **Dreamt by a woman** – you almost certainly harbour resentment concerning male behaviour towards you.
See also **Eunuch, Impotence**

Cats *See* **Animals**

Catastrophe

◆ ✄ **Participant or witness** – indicates that there will be a radical change in your situation.

✄ **Uninjured and helping** – the change will improve your condition.

✚ **Injured and unable to help** – a warning about taking chances.
See also **Accident**

Cave

● This is thought to represent the unconscious mind. Enter it and you may well encounter memories of times long past.

● **Being in a cave** – may reflect your desire for a sexual relationship or for a return to the safety and warmth of the womb.

Celebration

✄ ◆ A good omen for the future, especially for

those anxious about what is to happen, unless the event is unhappy.

Cell

♦ ● **Being locked in a cell** – you feel restricted in your waking life. For children this dream may express a wish for their parents to exercise greater authority.
See also **Prison**

Cemetery

● ♦ You are expressing a concern for deceased relations and friends, a fear of death itself, or a yearning for days long gone.
See also **Death, Funeral**

Chains

♦ **Being in chains** – you may feel that a heavy burden has been imposed on you.

♦ ● **Chaining another** – expresses a desire to control and possess someone who would not otherwise stay.

Chairs *See* **Furniture**

Chandelier

✖ **A shining chandelier** – presages success in business and private affairs.

♦ **A falling chandelier** – reflects your anxiety about a foolish action, or is a warning to exercise caution and judgment.

♦ **Hanging from a chandelier** – you are worried about putting something important to you at risk.

Chariots

✖ ✚ **Driving a chariot** – reflects some exciting and hazardous event in your life and may contain a warning against recklessness.

Chase

● ◆ **The dreamer who is being chased (by an animal or someone else)** – you are symbolically trying to escape from some unpleasant situation or unfortunate aspect of your own behaviour which it is difficult to face.

◆ **The dreamer chasing someone else** – expresses your aggressive impulses towards someone.
See also **Escape, Fear, Fugitive, Running**

Cherubs

✖ ◆ Indicate your positive feelings about children, or possibly an anxiety about the lost innocence of your own childhood.
See also **Angels**

Child/children

◆ **Self as a child** – you still, deep down, feel yourself to be immature.

● **Having fun with children, or a single child** – you are expressing an unconscious wish to have a family-orientated life.
See also **Adoption, Baby, Birth, Family, Parents**

Chilli con carne *See* **Food**

Chimney

◆ **Dreamt by a man** – you possibly fear impotence, even if subconsciously.

✖ **Dreamt by a woman** – an expression of feelings about your partner's sexual prowess.

Choking

◆ **The dreamer choking** – symbolic of a situation that is causing you tremendous worry. It may also sometimes be an expression of actual physical symptoms.

◆ **Choking someone else** – signals an unconscious desire to inflict harm on another.

Christ *See* **Jesus**

Christmas

✘ A prophetic dream of good times ahead.

Church

✘ **Exterior** – augurs well for the future.

◆ ● **Interior** – a sign of concern over religious beliefs and ideals, and a seeking after inner peace.

Circle

✘ ◆ The meaning of the circle is unity and wholeness, order and perfection. Should the circle be in any way incomplete or damaged, something is wrong.

◆ **Circular motion** – probably reflects a feeling that you are frustrated and 'going round in circles'.

✘ **Mandala** – represents the circle, with its unity and completeness. As a dream symbol, it may relate to the self and the dreamers attitude to him- or herself.

Circus

✘ **Watching a 'big top' act** – expect some surprises in the course of the next few days.

◆ **The dreamer as a clown** – you fear making a fool of yourself over a current relationship or situation.

Cleaning

◆ You should consider the possibility that you feel guilty.
See also **Dirtiness**

Clergy
● ✘ **Yourself as a member of the clergy** – you may want to become a better person or earn the respect and esteem of others.
● **Someone else as a member of the clergy** – perhaps you wish for an authority figure in your life or long for someone to aid and guide you.
● **Visiting the clergy** – you are in need of guidance and emotional support.

Cliff
♦ See yourself at the top of a cliff, looking down, and you undoubtedly fear some current situation.
See also **Abyss, Falling**

Climbing
● ♦ Indicates strong ambition in work, sex, socially or in ideals. If progress is difficult – and you slip back – the goal is too ambitious for you.

Clock
♦ **Ticking** – indicates a fear that time is short or even running out.
● **Winding up a clock** – you are anxious to make the most of every moment.
See also **Time**

Clothes
● **Buying new clothes** – you would probably like to change your image.
♦ ● **Taking off your clothes** – you either fear revealing some aspect of your personality or would like to shed a whole range of inhibitions.
See also **Nudity**

Clouds

◆ **Stormy clouds** – signify deep depression on the part of the dreamer.

⌘ **Fluffy white clouds** – indicate inner contentment.

Clown *See* **Circus**

Cockerel *See* **Birds**

Coffin

◆ **Dreamer finds self in a coffin** – you probably fear there is no way of escape from some situation, or realize deep down that you are at the end of a particular phase in your life.

◆ **Someone else in a coffin** – signifies guilt over some aspect of a relationship.

See also **Buried alive, Cemetery, Funeral**

Cold

◆ If the landscape is cold or icy, this indicates cold feelings towards others. If you are cold, it may mean you are frightened.

Collecting

⌘ Collecting things – stamps, coins, old objects – may mean a meeting with a celebrity.

Colours

Sometimes certain colours seem to predominate in our dreams and may in themselves be highly significant.

◆ **Black** – a predominantly black dream usually points to depression or general sadness.

● **Blue** – frequently signifies hopes for the future.

● **Brown** – symbolic of a sense of duty, and indicates a concern over what is right in a particular situation.

♦ **Green** – may signify jealousy or perhaps a concern with health and the environment.

♦ ♣ ● **Red** – may indicate anger, sexuality or a warning.

● **White** – symbolic of purity, usually pointing to a seeking after truth.

♦ ✖ **Yellow** – a pale shade mostly means well-being; darker tones may reflect a feeling of cowardice or treachery.

Comet
♦ Frequently indicates problems in life.

Computers
♦ You are probably concerned with the logical working out of some complicated emotional problem.

Conflict
♦ ✖ Become involved in any way in a conflict in a dream and it means there are problems and issues you are trying to hide. It is better to face them, overcome them or make peace than to continue the fight. The dream may show the solution.

Confusion
✖ **Attempts to remove muddle** – indicate that you will have an ordered and organized life.

♦ **Continuing muddle** – may stand for inner confusion.

Contentment
♦ May show that you are too little concerned about the troubles of others.

Cooking

✖ A contented home life is forecast. Or the dreamer may be transforming some inner conflict into something he or she can recognize and deal with.
See also **Food, Kitchen**

Corpse *See* **Death, Funeral, Morgue**

Corridor

◆ It is likely you are trying to escape from some restrictive situation in life.
See also **Alley, Road**

Cosmetics

✖ **For a woman** – a thoroughly positive dream, expressing contentment with your femininity.
● **For a man** – may express a yearning to change or to get in closer touch with your feminine characteristics.

Counting

✖ ◆ The act of counting is usually associated in waking life with money, so the dream could refer to the financial situation. Alternatively, the dreamer could be counting failures or blessings.

Cows *See* **Animals**

Crash

✖ **Any kind** – may mean some kind of achievement.
See also **Accident**

Crawling

● ◆ If you crawl in a dream, you would probably like to return to childhood. If you make someone else crawl, you may want to humiliate them.

Crescent

✖ ◆ Representative of the feminine – the emotional, irrational and mysterious. Perhaps this side of the dreamer has been ignored.

Crime

◆ ✚ **The dreamer committing crime** – Any crime indicates strong emotion. To kill means hate and to steal means desire. The dream may be expressing disapproval of inner impulses or warning you against some planned misdemeanour.

◆ **Someone else committing crime** – may reflect your distrust of someone, or the feeling that some wrong has been done to you.

See also **Burglary, Murder, Robbery**

Cross/crucifixion

● You are seeking comfort during a tricky period in your life.

See also **Jesus**

Crossroads

◆ **Being at a crossroads** – a clear indication that you have a decision to make, even if in waking life you wish to avoid it.

Crowds

✖ **At home in a crowd** – you will settle a long-standing difference.

● **Trying to escape from a crowd** – you are anxious to rid yourself of some restrictive relationship.

Crown *See* **Royalty**

Cucumber *See* **Food**

Curtains
♦ **Closed** – there is something preventing you from seeing the light and forging ahead.
● **Open** – you would like to make major changes to your lifestyle.

Cut
♦ A slash with any implement may mean the loss of a friend or of money.
See also **Knife**

Daddy Longlegs *See* **Insects**

Daffodil *See* **Flowers**

Dagger
♦ This could be a sign that, in waking life, you feel tremendous anger towards someone. Alternatively, you may suspect that someone is about to deceive you by taking advantage of your better nature.
See also **Aggression, Battle, Fight**

Dam
● **Building a dam** – the dreamer longs for greater control over his or her life.
♦ **A dam breaking** – expresses fear that things are going out of control.

Dancing
✖ Indicates joy, youth and victory, although there may be sexual associations, too.

Danger
✚ **Being in a dangerous situation** – may indicate that you should pay careful attention to finances and business matters.

Darkroom
✖ **Developing photographs in a darkroom** – you will solve a mystery that has bothered you for a long time.

Daybreak
✖ Predicts that you will find a way out of your difficulties and enjoy better times ahead.

Deafness
♦ **Unable to hear** – frequently a reflection of frustrated ambitions, or an unwillingness to face up to circumstances as they are.

● ♦ **Meeting with a deaf-mute** – symbolizes a genuine desire to do more to help the less fortunate. It may also be a sign that no one seems to be taking much notice of your needs right now.

Death
● **Finding yourself dead** – frequently an indication that you would like to leave behind all the world's worries.

♦ **Someone else's departing** – you probably greatly fear life without that person.

✖ **Someone who is dead** – you will shortly hear some surprising news.

♦ **Death of a parent** – may express subconscious rivalry between a son and his father or a daughter and her mother, and act as a safety-valve for angry feelings. *See also* **Bereavement, Funeral, Heaven, Medium, Morgue**

Debt
♦ **Running up debts** – you no doubt, deep down, fear loss of some kind, not necessarily financial.

✖ **Repaying debts** – a sign of forthcoming good fortune.
See also **Borrowing, Money**

Decay
◆ If decay – of buildings, food, etc. – is overpowering, this is a bad sign in all kinds of ways. Really facing up to difficulties and trying to solve them will help.

Deformity
◆ **Meeting someone with a deformity** – it may be that subconsciously you realize you should be more appreciative of your blessings in life than you are.
◆ **Having a deformity** – you are harbouring a guilty secret.

Deluge *See* Flood

Dentist
◆ **Having teeth pulled by a dentist** – this may be expressing a hidden fear of death.
◆ **Visiting a dentist** – you are struggling to come to terms with some unpleasant but necessary event or responsibility.

Depth
◆ Any dream of depth – water, a cave, underground – may mean that inner troubles are being suppressed.

Descending
◆ This means weakness. If the slope leads underground or to a cave, there may be inner problems to acknowledge and deal with.

Desert

♦ **Lost in a desert** – you feel in waking life that you lack a sense of direction.

✖ **Coming across a lush oasis** – predictive of wonderful news and a positive outcome to some difficult situation.

Desk *See* **Furniture**

Despair

✖ If the dream is full of despair, this may be a sign of improved fortunes.

Detective

♦ ● You are seeking a solution to some problem that has long been bothering you. Alternatively, you may be looking for greater recognition generally.
See also **Police**

Devil

♦ You are almost certainly feeling guilty, possibly about something quite minor that nevertheless still bothers you subconsciously. The devil may also represent a threat to your health.

Diamonds

✖ **Owning diamonds** – predictive of coming into good fortune.

♦ **Losing diamonds** – you are probably anxious about the stability of a relationship.

Dieting

♦ A dream of going on a diet may not, in fact, have

anything to do with reducing weight. Rather, it could be a sign that you will have to retrench due to financial problems.

See also **Obesity, Weight**

Dirtiness

♦ It could be that your subconscious is warning you about imminent ill-health. Alternatively, it may be that you are over-concerned about the face that you present to the world.

See also **Dust, Earth, Faeces, Washing**

Disappearance

✚ ♦ **Of a person** – predicts losses and even disaster, or suggests that your conscious mind does not completely understand something important.

♦ ✖ **Of an object** – you may be confused by problems, but should be able to cope with them.

See also **Invisibility**

Discipline

♦ The figure of authority who disciplines you in a dream undoubtedly represents your superego or the voice of conscience expressing its concern about past behaviour.

See also **School, Teacher**

Discovery

● Being 'discovered' and having some amazing talent recognized is an excellent example of a wish-fulfilment dream.

Disease *See* **Illness**

Disguise
♦ Likely to be a sign that you are trying to hide something or that you fear that someone is plotting against you in some way.
See also **Impersonation**

Dismissal
♦ Such dreams are increasingly common in times of economic recession and when jobs are hard to come by. They may, however, also reflect a fear of rejection by a loved one.

Disobedience
♦ A sign that you subconsciously resent certain restrictions in your life.

Distortion
♦ Dream scenes that somehow seem distorted – perhaps faces are overlarge or buildings remarkably small – usually represent an element of conflict that has arisen in waking life and has been bothering you over a long period.

Diving
● ✖ Could mean that you have been forgiven for some mistake, or it could indicate a desire to get to the bottom of a problem.
♦ This is most relevant if you are a non-swimmer and clearly indicates fear at having to face up to some desperate situation and anxiety about the outcome.
See also **Drowning, Falling, Swimming**

Divorce

✖ ◆ If you are happily married but find yourself
suddenly dreaming of going through the trauma of a
divorce, the chances are that your subconscious is
trying to remind you of how fortunate you are. Such a
dream could, however, also represent the break-up of
some other form of relationship – a business
partnership, for instance.
See also **Adultery, Infidelity, Marriage**

Doctor

◆ You should be taking greater care of your health or
are feeling rather neglected in waking life.
See also **Accident, Hospital, Illness**

Dogs *See* **Animals**

Doll

● Usually indicative of a desire to retreat to infancy,
when one was coddled and worries were minimal. Such
dreams may also point to a desire to have children of
one's own.
See also **Child/children, Puppet, Toys**

Door

◆ **Shut** – you feel isolated in some way.
✖ **Open** – take advantage of opportunities presenting
themselves.

Dove *See* **Birds**

Dragon

✖ **Meeting a dragon** – indicates forthcoming success
and great personal power.

♦ **The dragon attacks** – you are about to encounter a situation that will become overwhelming, for a fire-breathing dragon represents a feared figure of authority.

Dreaming

♦ To dream of having a dream is said to be a sign that you may have to be content with life as it is at present and put aside all ambitions and aspirations for a while.

Drink

⌘ **Fizzy** – sparkling drinks frequently signify a forthcoming celebration and exciting times ahead.
♦ **Hot** – if a drink scalds you in your dream, you are possibly fearful of the action that might be taken by someone towards you.
● **Milky** – this sort of drink often pinpoints a desire for renewed comfort from the mother-figure.
● **Warm** – a soothing warm drink sometimes signifies a yearning for sexual fulfilment.
● **Water** – cool, refreshing water could well be a sign that you are currently seeking spiritual awakening.
⌘ **Elegant drinking vessel** – great wealth in the offing.
See also **Alcohol, Drunkenness, Thirst, Wine**

Driving

● Whatever vehicle is being driven, the dream probably signifies a desire to control events, either through greater power for the dreamer or a wish to exert more control over others.

Drowning

◆ **The dreamer drowns** – frequently a sign that life is proving problematic, even overwhelming. Consider, too, whether there could be any connection with 'sinking' under pressing financial burdens.

◆ **The dreamer rescues someone from drowning** – you probably feel rather put upon of late.

See also **Diving, Falling, Swimming**

Drugs

◆ **Dealing in drugs** – consider carefully the motives of those with whom you socialize.

● **Taking drugs** – this is probably a sign of a desire for escape from a humdrum existence.

◆ **Heroin** – If you find yourself taking heroin or some other drug in a dream when, in waking life, you have never come into contact with such substances, you are probably feeling guilty about some aspect of recent behaviour.

◆ ● **Opium** – dreaming of taking opium does not indicate a wish to use drugs, but may arise out of boredom in your waking life, or express an unconscious urge to find peace during an excessively hectic period.

Drums

✘ ● Success is in the offing. Alternatively, it could be a sign that you feel in need of greater recognition.

See also **Music**

Drunkenness

◆ Dream of others being drunk while you remain sober, and you probably feel from past experience that

no one can be trusted but yourself, and fear being let down badly again.
See also **Alcohol, Wine**

Dungeon
● Reflects the desire to escape from a prevailing situation in waking life.
See also **Cell, Prison**

Dust
◆ **On the furniture** – indicates a concern about cleanliness and appearances.
✚ ◆ **Clouds of dust** – being surrounded by dust might mean you should anticipate minor irritations later on.

Dwarf
✖ **Meeting dwarves** – you are about to have some particularly enlightening experience.
✚ **Dreamer as a dwarf** – a warning that you should not put too much trust in others.
See also **Deformity, Distortion**

Eagle *See* **Birds**

Ear/earrings
✚ ● Your subconscious could be warning you to pay heed to a rumour you have heard. The ear is also representative of birth at times, in which case it may indicate a desire to reproduce. Dream of earrings and you should perhaps be more wary of initial impressions and take your time in getting to know someone properly.
See also **Deafness, Faces, Jewellery**

Earth

✚ Your subconscious is probably warning you to make careful provision for the future.

See also **Earthquake, Funeral, Garden, Grave**

Earthquake

✖ ◆ There could be a number of difficulties to overcome, or even a complete change of circumstances, for the better eventually.

See also **Volcano**

Eating

✖ The act of eating symbolizes love, strength and life. It is also a symbol of comfort.

◆ **Eating alone** – indicates feelings of loneliness and sadness.

✖ **Eating with others** – denotes improved fortunes and personal gain.

● **Sharing a meal with someone** – denotes a wish for a close relationship with that person. If sharing a meal with a member of the opposite sex, this indicates a desire for sexual intimacy.

See also **Banquet, Food, Restaurant**

Echo

◆ Likely to be a sign that you lack confidence in some area of life, or that you are currently in a rut and could do with a change of routine or environment.

Eclipse

◆ You could well be fearful that something will occur to put pay to a current relationship. Alternatively, the eclipse might symbolize feelings of being rejected and being placed very much in the shade.

See also **Moon, Sun**

Eggs *See* **Food**

Election

♦ You are possibly anxious about your popularity at work or on a social front and feel that you are constantly being assessed or judged.

Electricity

✖ Denotes good news from abroad.

Elopement

● You would dearly like to change your current circumstances or some unpleasant situation.

Embarrassment

✚ ♦ If you are embarrassed in a dream, you should be firm and not let others make you do something against your will.

Embers

♦ ● You may be harbouring fears of your own or someone else's death, or you may be wishing to end a business or personal relationship.

✖ **Rescuing something from the embers** – may denote a wish to help a friend in time of trouble.

✖ ● **Sitting with others around embers** – expresses pleasure at the company of your family or friends.
See also **Ashes, Fire, Fireplace**

Embrace

✖ ✚ **To embrace someone yourself** – indicates feelings of warmth and love for that person, but may contain a warning about the need for discretion to avoid public criticis

✚ **To see others embrace** – may be warning you that

criticism is coming your way, especially if you have recently received praise.

Embroidery

✂ **Seeing a woman embroider** – a predictive dream with the promise of innocent fun and some romantic adventures.

♦ **Embroidering something yourself** – may express doubts you have about your own conduct or that of someone near you.

Emerald

✂ ● **Seeing someone else with an emerald** – for women, this denotes a wish to receive that person's love; for a man, it expresses a desire for money.

✂ ● **Giving an emerald** – signifies the wish to give someone love or wealth.

✂ **Wearing an emerald** – augurs a happy future filled with love and prosperity.

Emptiness

✚ **Opening an empty container** – frustration. Don't undertake anything new, or it might fail.

♦ ● **Finding an empty room** – you may be fearful of loneliness or craving solitude.

♦ **Holding an empty glass** – expresses an anxiety about whether your life is as fulfilled as you would wish it to be.

Enema

● ♦ You are anxious to rid yourself of pent-up emotions. It may also be an omen of an unexpected drain on your financial resources.
See also **Faeces**

Enemy

◆ You fear a friend has turned against you for some reason. Alternatively, an enemy may sometimes symbolize a part of yourself that you find it difficult to face up to.
See also **Battle, Fight, War**

Engagement

● ✚ This could be pure wish-fulfilment. It may also be a warning from your subconscious that you should put some other matter entirely on to a firmer footing.
See also **Marriage, Ring, Wedding**

Engine

✖ You will probably accomplish much.
◆ **Repairing an engine** – expresses the feeling that something is amiss and needs sorting out.
◆ ● **Watching someone else repair an engine** – you may feel you would like help in dealing with some problem.

Epitaph

◆ Your subconscious could be telling you that you have perhaps not been as fair to others as you might have been.
See also **Death, Funeral**

Escalator

✖ **Going up an escalator** – likely to be an omen of success.
◆ **Going down an escalator** – you fear failure or loss of some kind because you have taken a major risk.
See also **Lift, Stairs**

Escape

● ✖ **To escape from a danger** – signifies that you want to make a change in your life, or denotes a rapid recovery from illness.

✖ **Seeing someone else escape** – financial matters should improve before long.

♦ **Something escaping the dreamer** – perhaps something important has been forgotten or misunderstood.

See also **Chase, Fugitive, Running**

Eunuch

♦ You feel very much in the hands of others during waking life and unable to do anything at all about the situation.

See also **Castration, Impotence**

Examination

♦ You feel under great pressure, with tremendous demands constantly being made of you at work, for it is not only students who experience such dreams.

See also **School**

Exchange

✖ ♦ The dreamer is about to experience a change in situation.

Execution

♦ ✖ **Your own execution** – you may be suffering depression or, as a compensation dream, you may have received a considerable reward for your efforts.

See also **Death, Hanging**

Exhaustion

✚ ♦ You are probably in need of a rest. Perhaps you

should look after your health and regain your energy.
See also **Fugitive, Illness**

Exhibition *See* **Museum**

Exhibitionism
● An indication that you would dearly like to throw caution to the wind.
See also **Nudity**

Exile
◆ ● **You are sent into exile** – you feel dissatisfaction with your life and may be considering foreign travel.
✚ **Another in exile** – a warning that quarrels may be on the way.

Expedition
◆ ✖ This is an omen of a long, severe struggle ahead, but one that may eventually bring reward.
See also **Travel**

Explosion *See* **Bomb, Earthquake, Volcano**

Eyes
The eye is a very potent dream symbol, representing many different facets of life, according to how it appears.
✖ **Beautiful eyes** – generally taken to be a sign of contentment or an omen of peace.
◆ **Closed eyes** – you may be failing to face up to the truth if your eyes will not open in a dream; whereas if you encounter closed eyes, it is probably an indication that you have suffered or fear rejection in waking life.
✚ **Crossed eyes** – be wary of someone you have recently met, the subconscious warns.

◆ **Disembodied eyes** – generally represent some threatening situation.

◆ **Injury to eyes** – you fear some major event that will upset general routine to a marked degree.

◆ **Squint** – you are unsure of someone's reliability.

◆ **Staring eyes** – you feel under duress in a work situation.

✖ **Winking eyes** – convey a message from your subconscious that you need not be taking life so seriously, and even perhaps that you might enjoy a mild flirtation.

See also **Faces**

Faces

Consider carefully the type you saw in your dream. The following list provides a basic guide to their symbolism.

● **Comic** – any form of cartoon face in a dream is generally regarded as a snub against society at large, whether conscious or unconscious.

◆ **Featureless** – the chances are that is precisely how you feel deep down: unappreciated and unnoticed.

◆ **Grotesque** – looming, ugly faces are most often a reflection of inner fears, quarrels or misfortunes.

✖ ● **Smiling** – there is a likelihood of financial gain. Alternatively, it may be a sign that you are striving for popularity among colleagues or friends.

See also **Ears, Eyes, Forehead, Mouth, Nose**

Factory

● Dreaming of a factory may signify a wish to 'manufacture' a new life for yourself.

✖ **Working in a factory** – augurs a busy and rewarding future.

Faeces

✖ **Encountering faeces** – an omen of wealth.
♦ **Incontinence** – you fear loss of self-control generally.
See also **Enema**

Failure

♦ ✖ May indicate that you should ask yourself if your aims can really be achieved. Or it could mean that if you approached your aims differently you could be successful.

Fairground

● You have probably been finding life rather restricting of late and would dearly love to let loose and have some fun.
See also **Amusement park, Merry-go-round**

Fakes

✚ Your subconscious is warning you against taking a gamble either in the love stakes or in business.
See also **Crime, Fraud**

Falling

♦ ✖ Generally reflects fear of failure at work or some other inadequacy. In other contexts, it may mean that the dreamer is yielding to some romantic or sexual temptation and may be 'falling' in love.
♦ **Hurt** – there could be difficulties in store.
✖ **Uninjured** – any upsets that do occur will be minor and just temporary.
See also **Abyss, Accident, Cliff, Stairs**

Fame

◆ ● You are anxious about ever achieving a long-held ambition that has not yet come to fruition. You are no doubt also seeking recognition for past efforts that you feel have been overlooked.

See also **Actor/actress, Applause, Film star**

Family

✘ **Happy family occasion** – bodes well for the future.

◆ **Family arguments** – often gross exaggerations of differences of opinion that may exist either in the family circle or at work.

See also **Adoption, Father, Incest, Mother, Mother-in-law, Parents, Siblings**

Farewell

◆ ✘ The chances are that you feel deep down that a relationship you value is about to come to an end, or that a move to another house is in the offing.

Farm/farmer

✘ **Prosperous farm** – an omen of financial gain and good health.

◆ **Poor farm** – prospects are not so bright.

See also **Animals, Earth**

Fashion show

◆ **Presence at a show** – the odds are that you feel inadequate as far as appearance is concerned.

✚ **Taking part in a show** – your subconscious is telling you that overconcern with looks is frequently an unattractive quality.

Father

♦ ✖ Dreams of your father can reflect your feelings towards him. Alternatively, you may be dreaming of an archetype that symbolizes authority and power, so that what happened in the dream refers to your attitude towards society as a whole rather than towards a parent.
See also **Family, Incest, Parents**

Fatigue

✚ Your subconscious is warning you of the need to take things rather more easily. Possibly, too, you are being advised not to take things too much to heart, and not to get upset by the foibles of others.
See also **Exhaustion, Illness**

Fear

✚ ♦ ● The overall emotion in a nightmare is fear. This acts as a warning to the conscious mind to investigate any hidden desires that may be making the dreamer feel guilty, or as a sign that the unconscious is trying to bring something to the surface. Other elements in the dream will provide clues to what the trouble is.
See also **Nightmares**

Feast *See* Banquet

Feather

✖ Some of your problems will become lighter in due course.

Feet

● Consider first whether you have been having any problems with your feet lately. If not, then your dream could symbolize a desire to 'find your feet' and make more progress on the work front.

● **Feet that itch** – indicates a desire to travel.

◆ **Cold feet** – an omen of unrequited love.

✖ ● **Bare feet** – signify delight in a new relationship, or that you seek a more down-to-earth existence, with less emphasis on the material things of life.

See also **Footprints, Nudity, Shoes**

Fences

◆ May indicate either that the dreamer is feeling enclosed, or that more privacy is desired, or they may represent self-control (too much, or lack of).

Fever

◆ ✖ You are either deeply concerned about some worrying matter, or possibly overexcited about the prospect of a forthcoming event.

See also **Illness**

Fields

✖ ◆ A symbol of peace and of 'green pastures', therefore of spiritual ease and grace. If the fields are brown, or left untended, the omens are less good.

See also **Meadows**

Fight

◆ To be involved in a fight probably signifies either moral or mental confusion. The circumstances of the dreamer will give clues.

See also **Aggression, Army, Battle, War**

Filing

◆ ✚ You are anxious about some form of disorder in your life. Alternatively, it could be a sign that you should compartmentalize your life more and not mix business with pleasure to such a degree.

Film star

● **Dreamer as a film star** – you undoubtedly desire greater attention.

● **Meeting a film star** – you would like to be accepted into a different social circle.

See also **Actor/actress, Audience, Fame, Stage**

Fingers

◆ **Pointing fingers** – you have a guilty conscience about something.

◆ **Varnished nails** – sometimes an omen of scandal.

● **Stroking or being stroked** – indicates a desire for a romantic or sexual entanglement.

See also **Hands, Manicure, Ring**

Fiord

✂ Dreams of narrow, mountainous bays and inlets are omens of peaceful, happy times at home.

Fire

◆ **House on fire** – you have feelings of intense anger towards someone.

✂ **Seated by a fire** – augurs well for a current relationship or family life.

✂ ◆ **Yourself on fire** – denotes that you are in the throes of an uncontrollable passion about which you may be anxious.

See also **Embers, Fireplace, Fire engine**

Fire engine

✂ An omen of successful escape from some difficult situation, but not necessarily anything life-threatening.

See also **Embers, Fire**

Fireplace

● **Elegant fireplace** – a desire to move up the social scale.

✖ **Cosy hearth** – a sign that great value is placed by the dreamer on family life.

See also **Embers, Fire**

First aid *See* **Accident, Death, Hospital, Nurse**

Fish/fishing

◆ To dream of fish may refer to the contents of the unconscious, or to cold feelings or impotence.

◆ ● **Acquiring a new fishing rod** – for a man to dream this denotes anxiety about his sexual powers; for a woman it could point to a wish for a new partner.

◆ **Catching fish** – you may feel a need to come to terms with some matter buried in the unconscious.

Fit

◆ **Seeing another have a fit** – denotes that family difficulties are leaving you at a loss to know what to do.

◆ **An animal having a fit** – signifies feelings of frustration and anger at work.

Flag

✖ **Flying banner** – you are likely to achieve success. Alternatively, if you are a rather reserved individual, your subconscious may be encouraging you to be a little more outward-going.

◆ **At half-mast** – ambitions are unlikely to be realized.

Flames *See* **Fire**

Fleece

♦ **Wearing something lined with fleece** – a period of trial and hardship is looming.

Fleet *See* **Ship**

Flint

● **Striking a flint** – you are probably in love and hoping for an early marriage.

Flirting

♦ **By a female dreamer** – you are probably behaving in a way that is completely contrary to your usual conduct during waking life – and one that you greatly resent in others.

⌘ **By a male dreamer** – your subconscious is allowing you to practise the art of flirting for benefit in waking life.

Floating

⌘ **With the current** – a sign of future prosperity.

♦ **Against the current** – your subconscious is expressing the view that you are too easily influenced. *See also* **Drowning, Sea**

Flocks of birds *See* **Birds**

Flogging

⌘ ✚ **Seeing someone flogged** – an omen that you will succeed in revenging yourself on someone who has wronged you; it may warn against unconsidered actions.

Flood

♦ **Victim of a flood** – you feel anxious about someone or a situation overwhelming you.

✖ **Escape from a flood** – your subconscious is telling you that you will both solve current problems and benefit from the experience.
See also **Drowning, Floating**

Flowers

Following Jung's theory about universal archetypes, certain types of flower may be representative of particular ideals.

◆ **Artificial flowers** – a sign that you mistrust some of your colleagues.

✖ **Daffodil** – augurs a time of hope, especially if you are experiencing troubles.

✚ ◆ **Lilac** – If you dream of lilac bushes or flowers it is an omen that illness will come to you or a friend, and that you are harbouring thoughts of death.

● **Lily** – concern about the afterlife.

● **Lotus** – a desire for greater self-knowledge.

● **Nasturtiums** – seeing nasturtiums shows a wish for new and interesting friends; eating nasturtiums, you may well soon decide to embark on an adventure.

✖ **Spring flowers** – optimism about the future.

Take careful note, therefore, about the sort of flowers you dream about, as well as whether they are in bud, full bloom, or past their prime.
See also **Garden**

Flying

● This is perhaps the most common of all dream topics. Such fantasies are said sometimes to have sexual significance, but this is not always the case. Indeed, such dreams frequently signify a desire to have

new experiences and a willingness to view the world from a different standpoint.
See also **Aeroplane**

Fog

◆ ✛ It is likely that you fear the possibility of something, or someone, standing in your way. Alternatively, your subconscious could be reminding you to look particularly carefully at the finer points in a contract, since you could lose out if their meaning is not clear to you.

Foliage

✖ **Green, fresh leaves** – denotes a happy romantic attachment and the prospect of marriage.

◆ **Brown, dead foliage** – you may be suffering disappointment in love or expressing the feeling that some aspect of your life is no longer satisfactory.
See also **Garden**

Food

● ✛ Dreams about food are generally highly symbolic and relate to one's emotional life. Try to remember the sort of foods you were eating in your dream – some, such as asparagus or oysters, have clear sexual significance. Asking yourself, too, whether they tasted sweet or bitter may provide further clues to a full and accurate interpretation of the dream.

◆ **Chilli con carne** – presages great upset in your intimate relationships.

◆ ● **Cucumbers (large)** – for a man this may reflect fears about sexual inadequacy; for a woman it could express a wish for the power and strength associated with masculinity.

● **Eggs, buying** – symbolizes a desire quite literally to conceive or to find creative inspiration.

◆ **Eggs, breaking** – may signify a need to get through to the truth about something.

◆ **Eggs, rotten** – generally an omen of ill fortune.

● **Jelly, eating** – may express an unconscious wish for pleasant interruptions to a dull routine.

● **Jelly, making** – you may be wishing for pleasurable reunions with old friends.

✖ ● **Lettuce** – dreams in which lettuce appears have a sexual connotation. If a woman gives a man a lettuce, she may be expressing her desire for intimacy. A man taking a lettuce from a woman indicates his yearning to conquer her.

✖ ✚ **Meat** – buying or eating meat is an omen that good fortune is in the offing. Frequently it also refers to the sensual side of life, or the sins of the flesh, and may contain a warning about immoral behaviour.

◆ **Meringue, eating** – you may harbour secret doubts about a colleague or friend, but they are lightweight and insubstantial.

✚ **Molasses** – eating molasses is an omen that you will be rebuked for making unwise statements. Be on guard in company, especially at work.

● **Muffins, baking** – you may be yearning for offspring: a 'bun in the oven'.

✖ **Muffins, eating** – indicates that you are enjoying good times with your family.

● ◆ **Mustard** – symbolic of faeces. Dreaming of spreading mustard is a sign of an unconscious wish to damage or destroy something or someone.

✖ **Mutton** – symbolizes cosy domestic bliss.

⌘ **Olives, eating** – a good omen portending to an unusual romantic episode.
⌘ **Olives, pressing for oil** – indicates that you are working hard for success in business or for love.
⌘ ♦ **Onions** – if you dream of many onions, this indicates that you will be successful but you will have to cope with envy and jealousy.
⌘ ♦ **Oranges** – interpretation depends on the actions in the dream, but oranges usually relate to feelings of sex and love. A tidy box of oranges signifies a well-ordered progress towards success. On the other hand, if in the dream you eat an orange, minor problems will slow down your progress.
⌘ **Parsley, eating** – a portent of enjoyable social gatherings.
⌘ **Parsley, picking** – you probably feel that the time has come to treat yourself to some small extravagance.
See also **Banquet, Menu**

Football *See* **Games**

Footprints
⌘ ♦ Your subconscious is considering whether or not it would be a wise move for you, literally, to follow in someone else's footsteps by entering a similar career or leading a similar sort of lifestyle.
See also **Feet**

Forehead
⌘ **A wrinkled forehead** – an omen of carefree, unworried times to come.
⌘ **Soothing someone's forehead** – reflects feelings of security and contentment with your partner.

Forest

♦ **Hiding in a forest** – suggests a guilty secret.
♦ ✖ **Plant and animal life** – a surprising event is imminent.
♦ **Lost in a forest** – symbolic of failure to find a satisfactory path in life.
See also **Foliage, Jungle, Tree**

Forgery

✖ An omen of money that will suddenly come to you from a surprising source, rather than an indication that there is a criminal side to your nature.
See also **Crime, Fakes, Fraud, Lies**

Fortifications

✖ Mean that you are successfully putting up defences against an enemy of some sort.

Fortune-telling

♦ ✚ You are probably fairly anxious about having to make a major decision in life. Your subconscious may also be recommending that you seek the advice of those you know you can trust, rather than a fortune-teller as such.
See also **Astrologer, Palm-reading**

Foundry

✖ ♦ If you dream of working in a foundry your subconscious may be suggesting that hard work and some suffering will prove constructive in the long run.

Fountain

✖ **Working fountain** – usually symbolizes happiness and freshness.

◆ **Broken fountain** – often refers to disease, old age and death.

Fragrance

✖ Any fragrant odour in your dreams denotes future promise and happiness.

✖ **Musk** – an omen of love and adventure.

See also **Odours**

Fraud

✚ **Dreamer committing fraud** – perhaps you should regard this as a warning about some of your actions and where they could lead. You are probably feeling guilty about something.

◆ **Someone else committing fraud** – probably the dreamer is too trusting.

See also **Crime, Fakes**

Freedom

◆ ✖ If the content of your dream is accompanied by a feeling of freedom you may be compensating for feeling trapped in your waking life. Alternatively, it may be an expression of satisfaction that everything is going well.

Freelance

◆ **The dreamer freelancing** – one of the worst omens, signifying that a life of unremitting and unrewarding labour will be yours.

◆ **Someone else freelancing** – you are expressing deep unconscious hostility towards that person.

Friends

✖ Indicates that you will enjoy a busy social life during the coming months. Often, too, it has been found that dreams of friends now living at a distance are followed by a communication from them in waking life.

Frost

♦ **Frostbite** – you feel that others have been rather cold towards you lately.
✖ **Frost on the ground** – could be an omen of a fresh start in some area of life.

Fruit

✖ **Ripe fruit** – probably indicates that your work is developing well or that your health could improve. It could also refer to sexuality.
♦ **Unripe fruit** – might mean poor health.
See also **Food**

Fugitive

♦ ● **Yourself as a fugitive** – expresses an unconscious desire to escape from conflicts at home, and perhaps your feelings of guilt about 'running away' from problems.
♦ **Helping a fugitive** – you may be harbouring feelings of disapproval about the conduct of a friend to whom you are under some obligation.
See also **Chase, Escape, Running**

Funeral

♦ Your subconscious is urging you to say goodbye to some aspect of life that you regret, rather than telling you about some imminent death.
See also **Death, Epitaph, Grave**

Fungus

♦ **A tree covered in fungus** – your subconscious may be alerting you to some problem with your teeth.

Funnel

✖ ● Dreams of pouring liquid from one container to another using a funnel have strong sexual connotations. You may be expressing your desire for an intimate relationship.

Furnace

✖ ✚ **Stoking a furnace** – an omen of passion entering your life or a warning of the need for industry to get you through difficulties.

◆ **An unlit furnace** – may express your sadness at not finding a suitable partner.
See also **Embers, Fire**

Furniture

● **Antiques** – often point to a desire to climb the social ladder.

● **Bed** – signifies a desire for greater emotional comfort. Dream of going to bed alone and the chances are you are over-tired or fear sexual rejection.

● **Bookcase** – you are probably seeking spiritual guidance.

● **Buying furniture** – you can be hopeful of a change in circumstances.

✖ **Chairs, comfortable** – you will receive an unexpected windfall.

◆ ✖ **Chairs, hard** – difficulties ahead will finally be overcome.

✖ **Desk, clearing out** – you will shortly encounter new and interesting situations or make new friends.

◆ **Desk, working at** – predicts that family troubles are coming your way.

◆ **Ebony furniture** – dream of ebony furniture and

you may well be heading for serious family quarrels
and disruptions.

✖ **Settee** – your subconscious is likely to be
encouraging you to pace yourself and make better use
of free time for leisure pursuits.

♦ **Shabby furniture** – you are probably feeling rather
embarrassed about some other aspect of life entirely.

● **Table** – you no doubt seek a relationship with firmer
foundations.

Furs

✖ You can hope for luxury and ease, or perhaps you
are already very comfortable materially.

Fury

♦ ✖ **Being in a fury** – your subconscious may be
alerting you to some injustice in your life.
Alternatively, the dream may be compensatory and
indicate that your waking life is very pleasing to you.

♦ **Someone furious with you** – you may feel you
deserve punishment for some action.

See also **Argument, Rage**

Fuse

● If a fuse blows in your dream, this could be a
symbolic play on words – indeed, you probably fear
blowing your top and releasing pent-up anger, yet
would dearly like to do so.

Gallows *See* **Hanging**

Gambling

♦ **Losing** – your subconscious is warning you against
taking unnecessary risks.

✖ **Winning** – this is not a sign that you should put money on a horse; rather, it is likely to signify a satisfactory outcome to some situation that has been bothering you.

✖ ◆ **Watching others gamble** – this denotes a wish to 'play safe' and perhaps expresses envy of those with the means or courage to take greater risks than you.
See also **Jackpot, Lottery, Luck, Money**

Games

✖ ◆ **Ball games** – may refer to sex. If a team is playing, this is how the dreamer sees life – as a game. If he or she is playing as an individual competitor, the dreamer is feeling resentful about having to cope alone, instead of enjoying the support of others.

◆ **Card games** – perhaps there is inner conflict about success.

◆ **Dreamer won't join in** – he or she is avoiding the game of life.

Gangs

● ◆ **Being a gang-member** – you may be expressing an unconscious wish for the approval and acceptance of others, or feeling that responsibilities are more than you can cope with by yourself.

◆ **Encountering a gang** – augurs a period of unrest and difficulty.

Garden

✖ **Beautiful garden** – an omen of tremendous happiness and abounding love. May also express nostalgia for lost innocence or youth.

✖ **Wild garden** – there may be difficulties ahead but

these will readily be overcome if you attend to them promptly.
See also **Flowers, Foliage**

Ghosts
♦ You are concerned about the effect that some action of yours has had upon someone else's happiness.

Giant
♦ You tend to not value yourself as you should and lack self-esteem.
See also **Growing, Ogre**

Gift
✛ ✖ **Receiving a present** – a warning from the subconscious against strangers bearing gifts, or a prediction of good luck.

✖ **Giving a present** – promises a happy outcome to present difficulties.

Girl
● ♦ For a woman to dream of herself as a girl may denote a longing for the past or express feelings of inferiority.

Glasses *See* **Spectacles**

Glassware
♦ **Breaking a glass** – an unconscious signal that a sharp domestic dispute is in the making.

✖ **Putting glass into a window** – an omen of future contentment and security.

Glider
✖ **Flying in a glider** – expresses positive feelings of

confidence and trust in your own ability to cope with
life and 'rise to the occasion'.
See also **Flying, Journeys**

Gloom

✚ A gloomy scene in a dream means the likelihood of
a headache.

Gloves

● **Putting on gloves** – if dreamt by a man, this has
clear sexual significance.
● **Buying gloves** – indicates the desire not to show
your hand and to keep something secret.
◆ **Losing gloves** – a fear of being discovered for what
one really is.
See also **Hands**

Glue

● May indicate a wish to bind someone or something
to you, or may mask your wish to be free.
◆ **Spilled glue** – likely to have a sexual connotation;
you may suspect a partner of infidelity.

Glutton

◆ **Being a glutton** – may augur that your success will
not bring you friends. It may also mean that you feel
your life is not 'nourishing' you in the way you need.
See also **Eating, Food**

Gnu *See* **Animals**

God

If you encounter God in a dream, it is likely that you
have recently come to terms with your mortality. For
some dreamers, however, God is clearly a symbol for

some figure of authority, such as an employer or teacher.

✚ **Worshipping God** – an unconscious message that you must get back on the straight and narrow.

✘ **Help from God** – your subconscious is reassuring you that things will work out in the end.

See also **Church, Heaven, Jesus**

Gold

✘ This may not in fact symbolize a concern with the materialistic things in life, but some valued, more abstract commodity, such as knowledge, beauty or compassion.

◆ **Losing gold** – an expression of anxiety or unhappiness over a lost opportunity.

See also **Money**

Golf *See* **Games**

Gossiping

◆ **Others gossiping about you** – reflects a concern that you feel overlooked in waking life.

● **The dreamer gossiping** – you are concerned about some aspect of your personality make-up that you would like to change.

See also **Jealousy**

Gourd

◆ ✘ ● A dream about this breast-shaped vegetable may indicate the desire for love and sex, or, if the gourd is old and shrivelled, could reflect a woman's anxiety about fading beauty.

Grandparents

◆ If you find yourself dreaming of grandparents who

are no longer alive, it is likely to be a sign that you are anxious as to what their opinion would have been about a particular matter or aspect of your life.
See also **Ancestors, Family**

Grass
✖ **Green and healthy** – a very good sign indeed for all areas of your life.
✚ **Withered and brown** – watch out for problems and illness.

Grave
◆ **Digging one's own grave** – a particularly nasty dream, signifying overwhelming current difficulties.
◆ **Digging someone else's grave** – you probably greatly regret some past action towards that person.
See also **Cemetery, Death**

Grease
◆ **Grease-stained clothes** – denotes anxiety at some foolish blunder.
◆ **Greasing machinery** – you may be worried that life and love are not running smoothly and that some action is needed to improve things.

Grief
✚ A health warning, perhaps for the digestion; you should take some action.

Grindstone
✚ **Turning a grindstone** – may express a warning that you should work harder, or resentment at how hard you have to work. It could also portend that you will suffer reverses but will triumph by persevering.

Growing

✖ Your subconscious is telling you that you are in fact capable of far more than you have achieved in life to date.

See also **Giant**

Guard

◆ If you dream of seeing a guard protecting something valuable, you may be worried about losing something close to you or feel that you are being kept away from what you desire.

Guest

✖ **Being a host** – implies achievement.

✖ **Being a guest** – probably means you will go travelling.

Guns

◆ ✚ A warning that you should try to be more open in expressing your emotions. Such dreams may also denote anguish concerning brutal or violent sexual behaviour.

See also **Weapons**

Gypsies

● Such dreams are generally symbolic of a desire for far greater freedom than a current lifestyle permits.

Haemorrhage *See* **Blood**

Hair

● **Long and flowing** – signifies a desire for greater freedom.

◆ **Having a haircut** – you feel that you are being restrained in some way.

✖ **Combing the hair** – denotes finding solutions to knotty problems. If you comb the hair of a member of the opposite sex, you will solve love troubles.
See also **Baldness, Barber, Razor**

Hall

◆ Signifies a period of anxiety if the hall is long and empty.

Halo

◆ ● You are probably going through a period of feeling inadequate. Alternatively, you may be seeking spiritual guidance.

Halter

◆ ● ✚ **Putting a halter on a horse** – indicates a feeling that you want to bring things under your control, or that you resent being under someone else's. In a punning sense, such dream may be warning you of the need to stop or halt some activity or person.

Hamlet

◆ A dream of a hamlet (small village) is an omen that you will meet with frustration. To dream of Shakespeare's character may indicate anger with a member of your family, especially a conflict with your mother.

Handbag

● **Looking in a handbag** – indicates a wish to penetrate into mysteries.
● ◆ **Losing a handbag** – an unconscious anxiety or desire concerning lost virginity.

Hands
◆ **Clenched fists** – represent repressed anger.
● **Extended hand** – symbolizes a need for friendship.
● **Stroking** – indicates sexual feelings.
See also **Fingers, Gloves**

Handyman
● ◆ **Employing a handyman** – portends trouble with a landlord. If a woman dreams this, it may contain a hidden desire for an intimate relationship.

Hanging
✚ **Dreamer as the executioner** – your subconscious is warning you about falling into the trap of being overcritical of others, lest you be judged for this yourself.
◆ **Dreamer is hung** – repressed guilt is probably coming to the fore.
See also **Death, Execution**

Hangover
✚ Your subconscious is warning you against the dangers of excess in many areas of life, not merely overindulgence in drink.
See also **Alcohol, Drunkenness**

Happiness
✚ ✖ If the mood of your dream is contentment, it may be a warning that you should look after your health. Children playing happily means good fortune. If you are experiencing grief or trouble, the dream may be a compensation.

Harbour
✖ An omen of future financial security.

✖ ● **Entering a harbour** – denotes success after possible difficulties along the way. For men, may have sexual overtones.

● **Leaving a harbour** – expresses the desire to break away from the routine and embark on adventures.
See **Boat, Yacht**

Harem

◆ **Female dreamer as part of a harem** – reflects lack of individuality or mistrust of someone with whom she is having a relationship.

◆ **Male dreamer as part of a harem** – the dream is unlikely to have sexual significance. Rather, the dreamer may be concerned about having to cope with too many things at once during the working day or be overwhelmed by family commitments.

● ✚ **Male dreamer owning a harem** – may be a simple fantasy or portend complications in work and private life.
See also **Adultery, Infidelity**

Harvest

✖ **Good harvest** – generally a symbol of forthcoming prosperity.

✚ **Poor harvest** – an omen of the need to cut back on outgoings.

● **Gathering a harvest** – for the childless, may express a wish to raise a family.
See also **Farm/Farmer**

Hat

✖ ◆ Likely to represent power or authority. In analysing the dream, take into consideration, therefore,

whether the hat was worn by or belonged to yourself or
someone else.

Havoc
✚ If you dream of havoc being caused by anything –
storms, war, burglary – it may be a warning from your
subconscious not to become obsessive about tidiness.

Hawaiian
✖ ● **In native costume** – may denote a wish for exotic
adventures or a message from your subconscious that
you need a good holiday.
✚ **Dressed as Europeans** – there are boring times
ahead.

Head *See* Faces

Hearse *See* Funeral

Heat
✖ **Comfortable heat** – indicates the passions and
maybe their passing with age.
◆ **Too much heat** – perhaps you should cool your
passions, which may be destructive.

Heaven
● ✖ Means either that you aspire to reach the heights
of ambition, that you probably aim for contentment and
peace or, more prosaically, that you have realistic
expectations of a better job.
See also **Angels, Death, God**

Height *See* Altitude, Falling

Hen *See* Birds

Hermaphrodite

✖ Usually has no sexual connotation at all. Far more likely, the dreamer is concerned about which way to go, having been presented with two distinct options.

Hermit

● Almost certainly a sign that you would like to have substantially more time to yourself.

Hero/heroine

● Consider the possibility that you are seeking greater recognition in your field of work.

Heroin *See* Drugs

Hiccup

◆ Your subconscious may be using a play on words, warning you that you could well experience a delay or 'hiccup' in your plans.

Hiding

● **The dreamer hides** – you would like to get out of the hustle and bustle of waking life.

◆ **An object is hidden** – you are concerned that someone is trying to take over your life.

Hill

This is a common setting for a dream and the significance may be in the actions of the dreamer.

◆ **Something or someone on top of a hill** – expresses the dreamer's fear or realization that the object or person is beyond reach.

◆ **Rolling down a hill** – anxieties about failing powers or a decline in health.

See also **Climbing, Descending**

Hitchhiking

✛ Your subconscious is warning you not to place too much reliance on others and to be more self-sufficient.

Hitting

◆ If hitting is involved in a dream, feelings of hostility, aggression and perhaps a fear of violence are being expressed.

◆ **Hitting another** – expresses your rage and destructive impulses.

◆ ● **Being hit** – may reflect an unconscious wish for punishment, or fear of the person hitting you.

See also **Aggression, Attack**

Hockey *See* **Games**

Hole

✖ ◆ Means the womb, or the vagina, and can therefore refer to being born. Alternatively, being inside a hole might indicate being in a mess.

✖ **Hole in clothing** – portends an improvement in your finances.

Holiday

✖ Your subconscious could be pointing out to you the benefits of having a break from routine.

Home

The interpretation of a dream in which the dreamer's home appears depends almost entirely on his or her situation and feelings about everything that means home.

Homesickness

✖ Probably you will hear from an old and good friend.

Homosexuality

✖ If such a dream comes as something of a surprise to you, it may in fact relate not to such a relationship but to the discovery of some other unexpected facet of your personality.

Honey

✖ An omen of recovery from illness or sweet experiences.

See also **Insects**

Honeymoon

✖ Such a dream is most likely to symbolize the cementing of a relationship, whether personal or business.

See also **Bride, Bridegroom, Marriage, Wedding**

Horizon

✖ **In the distance** – means success.

✚ **Near at hand** – you will have to cope with events that may mean problems for some time to come.

Horror

◆ ✖ The other elements in the dream must be considered carefully. However, the future may not be all that bad.

Horses *See* **Animals, Riding**

Horseradish

✖ A dream of horseradish denotes good fortune and the companionship of intellectually stimulating company.

◆ **Eating horseradish** – may express fears that others are laughing at your expense.

Hospital

✜ Your subconscious is warning you to relax and take things more easily.

See also **Doctor, Illness, Nurse, Operation, Surgeon**

Hostility

◆ **Towards you** – you are probably regretting some action.

◆ **Towards others by you** – you may be in a compromising situation.

See also **Aggression**

Hotel

◆ **Registering** – may mean greater responsibilities at work are causing you concern.

✖ **Living there** – your life may become easier and more secure financially.

✖ **Owning it** – you will most likely earn a fortune.

House

◆ **No door** – you feel you cannot escape a current situation.

◆ **In poor repair** – the dreamer feels emotionally bereft.

✖ **Childhood home** – relates to happy memories.

See also **Family**

Howling

✖ ◆ To dream that you or someone else is howling with pain or grief may indicate some serious emotional or physical upset in your life. As a compensation, it might indicate precisely the opposite.

Humidity

◆ **Being overcome by humidity** – expresses a fear of

being overwhelmed, either by circumstances, an enemy, or by passion.

Hunchback
✖ It has been said that the dreamer who sees a hunchback will be financially fortunate.

Hunger
✖ ♦ **You are hungry** – may mean that life will improve. Alternatively, you might not be happy at home.

✖ **You help someone who is hungry** – you will receive some financial benefit.
See also **Poverty**

Hunting
● **Joining a hunt** – you are preoccupied with achieving some goal you have set yourself.

♦ **Being hunted** – there is doubtless some worrying secret to be guarded.

● **Hunting for an object** – the meaning of such a dream depends largely on what is being hunted. If it is a key, the meaning may be sexual, or denote a problem for which you are seeking a solution.
See also **Searching**

Hurricane
♦ **Approach of a hurricane** – a clear dream of anxiety at some impending event.

♦ ✖ **Being caught up in hurricane** – may express fear or exhilaration at some thrilling or passionate experience.

Hypnosis
● You would like to relinquish the role of decision-maker for a while, and hand over such responsibility to someone else.

Hysteria
♦ **A woman having hysterics** – denotes family problems and business reversals.
♦ **Mass hysteria** – a dream of mob hysteria may reflect your anxieties concerning a national emergency or disaster.

Ice
♦ Dreams of ice may denote worries about death or sexual frigidity.
✖ **Sitting on ice** – paradoxically, this portends a life of comfort.
● **Slipping on ice** – you may be yearning for warmth and comfort, possibly a foreign holiday.
See also **Cold**

Iceberg
♦ You may be feeling blocked by obstacles at every turn in waking life. Alternatively, you may fear frigidity or feel that others are reacting particularly coldly towards you right now.
See also **Ice, Cold**

Ice-cream
✖ You are feeling particularly contented with life. As a predictive dream, it often indicates a forthcoming windfall.
See also **Food**

Idiot

♦ You are almost certainly either lacking confidence in some everyday situation or in need of letting go and freeing inhibitions.
See also **Asylum**

Idleness

✚ **Idling while others work** – a warning dream, alerting you to dangers at work; you may be called to account for something you have left undone.

Illegitimacy

♦ If you dream of suddenly discovering you were illegitimate, yet in reality you were not, this is a sign either of fear of losing your parents or of dissatisfaction with family life as it is.
See also **Family**

Illiteracy

♦ **Dreamer cannot read or write** – usually signifies extreme anxiety over expressing true, inner feelings.
♦ **Realizing someone else is illiterate** – an indication that you may have been treating someone unfairly.
See also **Reading**

Illness

✚ **Dreamer falls ill** – you would do well to consult a doctor. This is because the subconscious sometimes gives us a warning that something is awry before we are even aware of any symptoms. Also, watch out for arguments with those closest to you.
♦ **Someone else falls ill** – you should examine your attitude towards him or her, or possibly consider a fear of losing that individual's support.

Imagination

✘ If you meet someone with great imagination (such as a writer or artist), you will probably benefit financially from an inspiration of your own.

Immorality

✚ A warning that perhaps you should not judge the actions of others before you ensure that your own lifestyle is blameless.

Impersonation

● **Dreamer impersonates someone** – signifies a desire to escape from some present situation.
◆ **Someone impersonates dreamer** – you lack a strong sense of personal identity and feel that individuality is being suppressed.
See also **Disguise**

Impotence

◆ **In a man's dream** – the subconscious is expressing not some actual incapacity but deep concern about some other area of life, perhaps your career.
● **In a woman's dream** – you are expressing a desire to take a more dominant role generally in a relationship.
See also **Castration, Eunuch, Sexuality**

Impurity

✘ To discover impurities in your food, drink and suchlike is a portent of future happiness with a partner.

Incest

◆ This could be a sign that you are bothered about a completely different aspect of family interaction – in other words, the dream may have no roots in sex at all.

If, however, the dream keeps recurring and worries you,
you may wish to turn to someone for professional
guidance, through your general practitioner.
See also **Family, Sexuality**

Incubator

◆ You are probably concerned about the fragility of
some current situation, particularly as far as finances
are concerned.
See also **Baby, Birth**

Independence

✚ Should you demonstrate independence in your
dream, you may be in danger of being too sure of your
own abilities.

Indifference

◆ **Towards others** – it would be a good idea to ask
yourself if you do show indifference to people and if
this is what you want. You may end up with few
friends.

◆ **Towards the dreamer** – perhaps you should make
yourself more friendly and concerned in general, or
towards one person in particular.

Inferior person

◆ If you dream of someone who is inferior in any way,
consider if this person symbolizes the Shadow, the
inadequate side of your character.

Infidelity

◆ It may be that anyone who dreams of being
unfaithful should ask searching questions about the
present relationship.
See also **Adultery**

Inheritance

✖ **Substantial legacy** – generally taken to be a sign of good times ahead.

◆ **Meagre legacy** – an indication that you feel rejected.

See also **Money, Will**

Injury *See* **Accident, Hospital**

Inquiry

✚ **An inquiry you can't answer** – your subconscious is alerting you to the possibility that you may lose a friend.

Insects

◆ ✚ **Ants** – depending on your waking attitude towards ants, indicate a period of intense activity and hard work, anxiety about efficiency at work, or a warning that petty irritations may overwhelm you.

✖ **Bees, swarming** – the chances are that you will succeed at work as part of a team.

✚ **Bees, stinging** – be wary of the motives of others.

✚ **Bugs** – you will have to cope with something disgusting, and worse if the house is overrun with them. If you deal with them the outcome will be happier.

● **Butterflies** – symbolic of the spirit or psyche, a butterfly in a dream either represents the soul of someone once dear to you or a part of your being desirous of escape from worldly worries for a few hours.

✖ **Crane flies (daddy-longlegs)** – someone else being afraid of one is an omen that something amusing or pleasant will happen to you. Being frightened of one yourself, unless you suffer from a phobia of them, is a reassurance that something you dread is less fearful than you imagine.

◆ **Flies** – if you dream of irritating flies, you are probably experiencing the interference of others, much to your annoyance, in waking life.

✚ **Gnats** – may indicate that an illness of the nervous system is developing.

✖ **Moths, killing** – a dream which portends success in overcoming enemies.

◆ **Moths in your clothes** – expresses sadness at the destruction of something dear to you.

◆ **Spiders** – often symbols of cunning individuals who may be laying traps for you – in their webs. The web itself, meanwhile, is frequently representative of the complexities of life.

Insults

◆ **Received by dreamer** – you are likely to be harbouring guilt.

◆ **Given out by dreamer** – probably a sign of deep anger towards someone that has never been outwardly expressed.

Intercourse

● **Dreamer makes love** – likely to be pure wish-fulfilment.

◆ **Witnessing others making love** – you may well be holding back some emotional problem that needs resolution.

See also **Impotence, Love, Sexuality**

Intestines

✚ ◆ If you dream of your own intestines, your

subconscious may be drawing attention to something wrong. If there is pain in the dream, you may be wise to seek medical advice.

Invalid

♦ **Dreamer as invalid** – means unpleasant circumstances.
♦ **Others as invalids** – could be a sign that unpleasant people are interfering with your activities.
See also **Illness**

Invisibility

♦ The chances are that this is very much how you feel in everyday life – overlooked and undervalued.

Invitation

● **Dreamer receives invitation** – a form of wish-fulfilment, indicating that you would like to extend your social circle.
● **Dreamer sends out invitation** – could be an underlying plea for help.
See also **Letter**

Ironing

● What you are doing in your dream probably reflects that you would dearly love to 'smooth over' current difficulties in everyday life.

Island

⌘ ♦ Islands can mean isolation, loneliness, escape, paradise, a firm place to be in a sea of problems, or all of these.

Itching

✚ ♦ You may soon be irritated by minor problems.

Jackpot

● Your subconscious is trying to find a way out of current financial difficulties for you.
See also **Gambling, Lottery, Money**

Jack-knife

◆ **Dreamer has a jack-knife** – may denote anxieties about being considered two-faced by friends or acquaintances.

◆ **Someone else has a jack-knife** – you may want to ask yourself if you really trust that person.

Jail

● ◆ **Dreamer in jail** – you are feeling confined in some way, or you want to confine some of your feelings. Alternatively, it can mean a belief that you should be punished, or fear that you will be punished for some bad action. If children dream they are in jail, this may mean they want their parents to exert more discipline.

● ◆ **Dreamer as jailer** – means the dreamer wants to restrict others or be the boss.
See also **Cell, Prison**

Jaws

◆ You fear having your needs and ambitions swallowed up in favour of those of others.

Jealousy

✚ **Dreamer encounters jealous individual** – your subconscious may well be warning you about forthcoming problems on the relationship front or perhaps at work.

◆ **Dreamer is jealous** – reflects a general feeling of inadequacy in waking life.
See also **Colours**

Jelly *See* **Food**

Jerusalem
● You are hankering after spiritual guidance, symbolically seeking to resolve a controversy in your life, or perhaps simply expressing a desire to visit a place that has always been a source of fascination to you.

Jesus
● **Encounter with Christ** – you are almost certainly seeking religious commitment.
◆ **Crucifixion** – you are experiencing undue guilt.
See also **God**

Jewellery
● ✖ Since jewellery represents value, jewels appearing in a dream can mean love to a woman and wealth to a man. They also stand for integrity, an individual's sense of oneself, and sexuality. The interpretation depends on the concerns of the dreamer.
◆ **Jewels turning out to be glass** – probably means the shattering of an ideal.
See also **Ear/Earrings, Necklaces, Ring**

Joke
◆ **Dreamer as victim of joke** – a sign that you fear being taken advantage of.
✖ **Dreamer plays practical joke** – predictive of a successful outcome for some business venture.

♦ ● **Dreamer tells a joke** – examine its content carefully. Some aspect of its subject matter is probably bothering you right now and you may well wish you could simply laugh off the situation.
See also **Clown**

Journeys

The path of life, with its obstacles and joys.
⌘ **Accident avoided** – a skilfully controlled escape stands for sufficient control over the emotions.
⌘ **Aeroplane** – a rapid progress towards aims.
⌘ ♦ **Arrival** – indicates achievement or good health, or in old age can represent death.
● ⌘ ♦ ✚ **Bicycle** – usually refers to adolescence. Can also be interpreted sexually or as a sign that you are having to make great personal endeavours to succeed. Riding a bicycle downhill is a warning dream alerting you to potential dangers ahead.
● ⌘ ♦ **Boats** – in dreams these stand for the boundless possibilities of travel by water. If you are rowing hard, the likelihood is that you are resentful of having to put so much effort into life. If you are in a boat out at sea, you feel that you have lost direction in life.
● ⌘ ♦ **Bus** – the journey of life here refers to short periods.
● ⌘ ♦ **Car** – often a symbol of sexuality. Speeding can represent sexual misconduct; being unable to stop can indicate fear of taking risks, lest there is no turning back. Faults in the steering or breaks might mean a lack of control or discipline. Driving usually indicates desire; being driven can indicate dependence on

someone else. Driving without a licence means you have some guilty secret or a fear of authority. Overtaking implies taking masterful control of events.

✚ **Crashes** – arguments are on the way.

◆ **Future hindrances** – perhaps blocks to ambition should be recognized, especially if they are of the dreamer's own making.

◆ **Missing a vehicle** – dreams in which an aeroplane, bus or train are missed usually indicate physical tiredness, lack of energy, a failure to understand or order life efficiently or missed opportunities.

● ✖ ◆ **Motorcycle** – a male sex symbol. Riding a motorbike means a successful and happy sexual relationship. Crashing a motorbike may indicate a subconscious desire to terminate a relationship or to express fears about it ending.

◆ **Past obstacles** – related to difficulties, past and present.

✖ ◆ **Roads** – signify an individual's own path of life, with all the hazards and disappointments illustrated relatively obviously in the dreamer's journey.

● ✖ ◆ **Train** – may give clues about the energy of the dreamer, his or her drive and sexuality. Trying to get off a train often means a desire to slow down or avoid reaching journey's end. In a man's dream, a train has sexual significance, particularly if entry into a tunnel is involved. In a woman's dream, a train means she would like to take on a more dominant role.

◆ **Turning a corner** – fundamental changes may be taking place.

✖ **Walking** – deliberate walking in a dream signifies a

desire to proceed towards all ambitions slowly and under one's own steam.
See also **Accident, Travel**

Judge

♦ You are feeling guilty about some misdemeanour, however minor. You may be feeling guilty quite unnecessarily, but your subconscious insists that you play fair.
See also **Accusation, Jury**

Juggler

✚ ♦ Reflects a need to examine your finances rather carefully. It may also indicate that you have been doing rather too much of late.

Jumping

✖ ♦ You are probably very successful, unless you fail, in which case things can be very disagreeable.
See also **Leaping**

Jungle

♦ **Impenetrable vegetation** – you are anxious about what the future holds for you.
● **Exploration** – your subconscious yearns for a change of waking environment.
See also **Foliage, Forest, Tree**

Junk

✚ If your dream contains a pile of rubbish, you may find it difficult to make a decision in the near future.

Jury

♦ **Dreamer as part of jury** – you are questioning, subconsciously, your very role in life.

◆ **Dreamer on trial before jury** – you are probably concerned about the reaction of family and friends to some course of action you have taken.
See also **Accusation, Judge**

Karate

◆ The chances are that you feel you need to defend yourself against some sort of opposition, either within the family circle or perhaps at work.
See also **Aggression, Fight, Kicking**

Kettle

◆ If you dream of a kettle on the boil, that may be precisely how you feel inside: almost ready to explode and all steamed up with anger for some reason.

◆ **A broken kettle** – may well signify that you see great obstacles in your path and will need to struggle to achieve your goal.

Key

◆ ● A key in a dream can mean many things. For example, the dreamer is looking for a solution, wants help in overcoming a problem of inferiority, is searching for a key to remove an obstacle, wants to be accepted sexually or wishes to hide from intrusion.
See also **Lock**

Kicking

◆ **The dreamer is kicked** – you are having to face up to serious opposition in waking life.

● **The dreamer kicks out** – you feel like getting your own back on someone.
See also **Aggression, Fight, Karate**

Kidnap *See* **Abduction**

Killing *See* **Murder**

Kindergarten
♦ It is likely that you feel that those around you in waking life have been acting rather childishly of late.
See also **Child/children, School**

King *See* **Royalty**

Kiss
● **Dreamer kissing** – you are expressing feelings that you hesitate to show when awake.
✖ **Kissing between couples and of children** – happiness and success will be yours.
✖ **Kissing your partner** – a sign of harmonious love.
♦ **Insincere kissing** – a sign of illness or disgrace.
✖ ♦ **Strangers kissing** – could mean conquest.
♦ **Your partner kissing another** – you may be harbouring unconscious fears about infidelity, or a secret wish to separate.

Kitchen
✖ ● **Lavish preparations** – you can probably expect some good news soon. Alternatively, it may be a sign that you are anxious to impress in waking life for some reason.
♦ **Dilapidated surroundings** – may be a reflection of the state of your emotions.
See also **Baker/baking, Banquet, Cooking, Food**

Kite
✖ An omen that you will achieve your life's ambition before too long or manage to break free from some restricting situation.
See also **Flying**

Kitten *See* **Animals**

Kneeling

◆ **Kneeling in inappropriate places** – a dream of kneeling in say, the supermarket, car park or some other unsuitable location may well point to an unconscious wish to atone for some real or imagined wrong.

Knife

◆ **Sharp knife** – signifies the prospect of vengeance, family squabbles or even a deathwish.
✚ **Cutting self** – a warning that actions you have taken lately will prove to your detriment.
See also **Accident, Blood, Cut, Murder, Suicide, Weapons**

Knight

● You probably seek someone to protect you and look after your needs.

Knitting

✘ A symbol of domestic happiness and the blessings of children.

◆ **Dropping stitches** – represents loss of money.
◆ **Tangled wool** – involvement in family problems lies ahead.

Knocking

◆ **By the dreamer** – you may have to ask for advice.
◆ **Heard by the dreamer** – you will probably receive some serious news.
◆ **Repeated knocking** – may express a feeling of frustration that you are being ignored. Could have a factual basis in noisy surroundings.

Knots

✖ **Dreamer tying knots** – shows an independent and firm nature.

◆ **To see knots** – the dreamer is likely to be a worrier.

◆ **To try to undo knots** – if the dreamer fails, this indicates anxiety about lack of self-control.

Ku Klux Klan

✚ ◆ **Self as member** – may be a warning not to involve yourself in plotting or devious undertakings.

◆ **Another as member** – you may wish to look closely at someone your subconscious portrays in this way.

Laboratory

● ◆ Perhaps you want to expand your scientific interests. Alternatively, you may be anxious to test somebody, or worried because you feel you are being tested.

● **Experimenting in a laboratory** – you may be feeling unhappy with your present life and wanting to experiment with new ideas or people.

◆ ● **Looking at a laboratory** – may express hidden envy of those whose affairs are in order, or a desire to emulate them.

See also **Scientist**

Labour *See* Birth

Labyrinth

◆ Find yourself lost in a maze and you are likely to find it difficult to untangle a complex problem, possibly one of your own making. Should there be wild beasts to add further dangers, you are probably suffering from obstacles put up by those who wish you ill.

Lace

● Dreamed of by a woman, indicates a wish to be prized for her femininity. A man dreaming of a woman in lace may need to recognize his sexual feelings for the person concerned.

Ladder

◆ **Climbing a ladder** – reflects your aspirations for promotion at work and a wish to reach the top.

◆ **Descending a ladder** – perhaps you are aiming too high. A disappointment may be in store for you.

◆ **Falling from a ladder** – you lack self-confidence.

◆ **Entering a house by means of a ladder** – a portent of an unwelcome message.

See also **Falling**

Ladle

◆ **Serving food with a ladle** – may express hidden resentment at having to look after others, particularly uninvited guests.

Lady

◆ Meeting a woman with the title 'Lady' may be a disapproving judgment on her by your subconscious.

Lagoon

✘ The still, mysterious waters of a lagoon are a powerful symbol of female sexuality, especially if the dreamer is male.

◆ **Drowning in a lagoon** – expresses serious sexual anxieties.

See also **Lake, Water**

Lake

✖ **Calm waters** – augurs well for your love life.

◆ **Stormy water** – generally an unfavourable omen.

✚ **Monster in the waters** – your subconscious is warning you about possible competition in the emotional stakes.

See also **Lagoon, River, Water**

Lameness

◆ ✖ Almost certainly you fear that some obstacle will hinder you from succeeding. Your subconscious could also be trying to tell you that often it is possible to make major achievements in spite of difficulties standing in the way.

See also **Amputation, Deformity**

Lamp *See* **Light**

Lamppost

◆ **A broken lamppost** – indicates a disagreement with a neighbour.

Lance

If a man uses a lance on a woman, the dream is clearly sexual and may indicate his wish for intimacy.

◆ ✚ **Having a boil lanced** – a warning from the subconscious that an uncomfortable situation or relationship can be solved only at great cost to yourself.

Landing

● ✖ Whether in a ship or an aeroplane, dreaming of landing indicates the desire to achieve your goal safely, or satisfaction at having done so.

See also **Journeys**

Lane *See* **Alley**

Language

● Should you find yourself confronted by people talking in a foreign tongue – one you do not speak in waking life – this is almost certainly a sign that you would like to broaden your horizons.
See also **Accent**

Lantern

● Dreaming of lanterns may reflect a wish to find out the truth about something, or for 'enlightenment'.
◆ **Signalling trains with a lantern** – an omen of trouble to come.
See also **Light**

Lapdog *See* **Animals**

Lapis lazuli

✖ Dreams about this beautiful blue gemstone augur happiness and a contented married life.

Lard

✚ ◆ **Cooking with lard** – dreams in which you cook with lard indicate an unconscious worry about the reliability of a colleague or friend – you may secretly feel they are 'greasy' or 'slippery customers'.

Lasso

✖ An omen of wealth that will be coming to you.

Lateness

✚ Arrive late for an appointment in your dream and your subconscious is warning you against making plans without careful forethought.

Lathe
♦ ● **Turning wood on a lathe** – often reflects concern over a plan or project; you may be looking forward to its success or worried that it might fail.

Lattice
✖ ♦ **Opening a lattice window** – if the scene is pleasant and beautiful, it expresses your confidence about your life at present; if the scene is ugly or frightening, it indicates your anxiety.

✖ ♦ **Climbing through a lattice window** – a sign of your eagerness to embrace the future, or possibly your dread at the inevitable.
See also **Window**

Laughter
♦ **Unwelcome laughter** – you no doubt are rather worried about the fact that a proposition you have made, perhaps at work, will not be given the attention you feel it deserves.
Welcome laughter – reflects a desire on your part for greater popularity among colleagues.
See also **Clown, Joke**

Launch
● ✖ The launching of boats or ships denotes a yearning for a new departure, and frequently presages exciting adventures.

Laundry
♦ You are concerned that some guilty secret will leak out.
See also **Washing**

Laurel

● **Wearing laurel yourself** – the association of laurel with victory means that this dream is pointing to a wish to succeed or a desire to have your achievements noticed and celebrated.

◆ **Another wearing laurel** – you may be feeling that a friend or rival is coming out on top.

✖ **Laurel seen on a bush** – you will meet success in an important undertaking.

Lava *see* **Volcano**

Law *See* **Judge, Jury**

Laxative

◆ You are worried subconsciously about your performance in some particular area of life.
See also **Enema, Faeces**

Laziness

✚ If, as a rule, you are extremely active and diligent, your subconscious could well be warning you that the time has come to take things a little more easily.

Lead

◆ **Carrying a load of lead** – indicates feelings of being put upon, and is an omen of troubles ahead.

Leak

◆ If you see a leak, you are probably grieving over a loss.

✚ **A leak in your shoes** – a warning to look after your health.

◆ **Leaking tap** – you may be regretting having spoken out of turn or spreading a rumour.

Leaping

✖ ◆ **Leaping over an obstacle** – if your leap is successful you are likely to succeed in your aims; if unsuccessful, you may need to work harder to reach your goal.
See also **Jumping**

Learning *See* **School**

Leper

◆ A portent of struggles that lie ahead. Dreams in which a person you know becomes a leper express your anger or ill will towards that person.
See also **Deformity, Illness, Lameness**

Letter

● **Dreamer writes a letter** – indicates a desire to communicate more successfully.
✖ **Dreamer receives a letter** – you will gain financially.
◆ **Reading someone else's letter** – an omen of financial loss.
See also **Invitation**

Lettuce *See* **Food**

Library

✖ Your subconscious is trying to come to terms with some new idea or piece of knowledge. It is also sometimes a fortunate omen, indicating some forthcoming fascinating discovery.
See also **Book, Illiteracy, Reading**

Lice

◆ **Being infested with lice** – for a woman to dream of

getting infested with lice expresses her unconscious horror at the thought of pregnancy and having unwanted children.

● **Killing lice** – indicates a wish to rid oneself of undesirable and troublesome difficulties.

Lies

✖ **The dreamer hearing lies** – would seem to indicate something bad, yet it usually augurs well for the future, particularly in matters concerning money.

✖ ◆ **The dreamer telling lies** – if, in waking life, you are truthful, expect some event that will change your outlook on life completely. Alternatively, it may be that you have recently acted in some way that is quite out of character, and your subconscious has chosen to point this out to you in a poignantly symbolic way.

Lifeboat

◆ ● **Lifeboat going to the rescue** – expresses your feeling that you need rescuing from some situations, or perhaps that you wish to rescue someone else.

◆ **Lifeboat overturning** – a sign of serious trouble ahead from an unexpected source.

Lift

✚ May represent a message that your unconscious is trying to bring up into your waking mind.

◆ **Riding up and down in a lift** – frequently indicate a secret dissatisfaction with one's sex life, which you may feel has become mechanical and dull.

◆ **Getting stuck in a lift** – signifies worries about death.

Light

⌘ A fortunate omen, signifying the resolution of some difficulty.

⌘ ♦ **Light coming from a particular place** – your unconscious is trying to direct your waking mind towards what lies in that direction.

✚ **Dim and insufficient light** – a message that you are not aware enough of something, or have not understood something properly.

✚ **Blinding light** – you may be paying too much attention to your conscious mind and are missing out on the wisdom of your intuitive side.

See also **Lighthouse, Lightning, Rainbow, Sun**

Lighthouse

✚ ● Freudians believe such a dream has a strong sexual significance. It also sometimes signifies that the dreamer is seeking escape from some stormy relationship.

Lightning

⌘ **Flashes of lightning** – a sign that you will shortly find out the truth concerning something that has long been bothering you.

✚ ⌘ **Lightning rod** – your unconscious is offering you a warning about dangers from an unforeseen source, yet is also assuring you of your ability to cope.

⌘ ♦ **Struck by lightning** – you will soon come up with some wonderful invention or idea. If you are transformed by the lightning, this indicates a change being wrought by sudden knowledge, such as a religious conversion or realization concerning a partner.

Lilac *See* **Flowers**

Linen
● **Table linen** – you wish to improve your social standing.
● ✖ **Bed linen** – reflects your yearning for love, and is a good omen in terms of romance.
● **Clean linen** – a sign that you have, or would like to have, a clear conscience.

Lions *See* **Animals**

Lips
✖ **Attractive lips** – happy circumstances.
✚ **Unattractive lips** – beware of troubles.
See also **Faces, Kiss, Lipstick**

Lipstick
● ◆ **Putting on lipstick** – this has fairly strong sexual overtones; you may be longing for sexual intimacy or fearing it, depending on how you feel in the dream.
See also **Lips**

Litter
◆ A sign that your emotional life is in something of a mess right now.

Lock
● **Unlocking a door** – sexual connotations, if dreamt by a woman.
◆ **Someone picking a lock** – indicative of a feeling that someone has been meddling in your affairs, much to your annoyance.
◆ ● **Locking someone in a room** – expresses your jealousy and desire to keep that person all to yourself.

◆ **Locking yourself up** – you are afraid of being harmed by letting others get close to you.
See also **Door, Key**

Locomotive
◆ Because it is a symbol of power, to dream of a locomotive usually means the dreamer fears being not powerful enough and wants to be stronger.
See also **Journeys**

Logs
✄ **Sawing logs** – portends home comforts and domestic satisfaction.
✄ **Sitting on a log** – reflects your satisfaction with the small things in life.

Lollipops
✄ ● Because of their strong association with the pleasures of childhood, dreaming of lollipops indicates nostalgia for the past and perhaps a need for comfort and consolation.

Loneliness
● You probably have very little time for yourself and yearn for greater privacy.

Loom
● ✄ **Weaving cloth on a loom** – you may be longing for greater order in your life, or happy with the pattern of events.

Loss
◆ **To lose something or getting lost** – signifies mental distraction or lack of concentration.
✚ **Loss of reputation** – illness may overtake you.

✖ **Finding the lost object or the way** – the difficult period is now over.

Lottery

● The chances are that you are in financial difficulties and that this is pure wish-fulfilment.
See also **Gambling, Jackpot, Luck, Money**

Loudspeaker

◆ **A blaring loudspeaker** – reflects your frustration at having your feelings or ideas 'drowned out' by others.
✖ **Turning down a loudspeaker** – a sign that you are prepared to assert yourself.

Love

● A dream of true love and companionship between a man and a woman, not necessarily featuring the dreamer, but possibly complete strangers, is generally an example of wish-fulfilment.
See also **Intercourse, Kiss, Marriage, Wedding**

Luck

✚ **Having good luck** – your unconscious may be warning you not to take things for granted and to keep striving towards your goal.
◆ ✖ **Having bad luck** – you may be feeling hard done by or envying someone who has been more fortunate. Frequently, dreams of ill luck portend a change for the better.

Luggage

◆ **Dragging heavy baggage** – symbolizes the problems we all have, however petty, that sometimes drag us down.

✄ **Losing luggage** – an omen that the effect of this burden, whatever it is, will soon lighten.
See also **Journeys, Travel**

Lunch *See* **Restaurant**

Lust
✚ Be very careful of your behaviour if you dream of giving way to lust.

Luxury
✚ If you dream of luxurious living, this is a warning that you should keep on working hard.

Lyre
✄ **Playing a lyre** – presages romantic love (someone to make beautiful music with).
♦ **A tuneless or broken lyre** – denotes dissatisfaction with your working or domestic arrangements.
See also **Music**

Machinery
Very often this is a symbol for the body and especially the brain.
✄ **Taking machinery to bits** – fiddling with machines may represent an attempt to correct a fault in the inner workings of the mind.
● ✄ **Well-oiled machinery** – you may be wishing for your life to run smoothly, or pleased that it is.
✚ **Rusting machinery** – may be a warning to look after your health.
See also **Engine**

Magic

✚ **Watching a conjuror** – your subconscious is warning you against being taken in by a confidence trickster.

✖ **Dreamer as the magician** – an omen of some wonderful event that will shortly occur.

Maid

♦ ● **Employing a maid** – you are in need of someone to rely on right now. Alternatively, you may be yearning for someone to take your guilty burden off your shoulders.

● ✚ **Employed as a maid** – an expression of your eagerness to help others and a warning to take care lest others use you in some way.

Mail *See* **Invitation, Letter**

Mandala *See* **Circle**

Manicure

✚ Your subconscious is warning you to take greater care of yourself.
See also **Fingers, Hands**

Manna

✖ **A dream of manna from heaven** – this reconstruction of the biblical experience of the Israelites in the desert is an omen of a financial windfall.

Mansion

✖ **Living in a mansion** – portends a happy domestic life or may be simple wish-fulfilment.

Map

◆ **A confusing chart** – a sign that, in waking life, too, you lack a sense of direction.

✖ **Following a map** – you are likely to embark upon new and successful plans shortly.

See also **Navigating, Travel**

Marathon

◆ ✚ **Running a marathon** – for non-athletes this denotes frustration at being asked for too much at work and a warning to take things easier.

✖ **Winning a marathon** – you have probably come through a difficult period in your life.

Market

✖ ◆ An omen of prosperity if the foodstuffs on display are ripe and tempting; if they are wilting and unattractive, the omen is bad. Alternatively, your subconscious may be reminding you that you have to make a series of choices.

See also **Shopping**

Marriage

● If, in waking life, you are single, this could be pure wish-fulfilment. It may also represent that, as far as work is concerned, you are in need of a partner.

See also **Adultery, Bride, Bridegroom, Divorce, Wedding**

Marsh

◆ **Walking through a marsh** – denotes that a period of ill health or other misfortune may be on the horizon for you.

Mask

In dreams, masks usually stand for your persona or facade, the face you present to the world.

✖ **Attending a masquerade** – and you could well find yourself embarking on a romantic adventure.

♦ **Mask worn by someone else** – you fear that a certain individual's motives are not genuine.

♦ ✚ **Dreamer wears a mask** – you have something to hide, either by way of an emotion or some past misdemeanour. If you can't take the mask off, you are being warned that your persona is taking over your real self.

See also **Disguise, Faces, Impersonation**

Massage

● ✚ You crave more physical contact. It may also be that your subconscious is reminding you to look after your health more carefully.

Match

✖ ● **Striking a match** – may denote the beginning of a special relationship, or be an expression of yearning for a partner.

Mathematics

♦ **Insoluble problem** – if you dream that you are unable to solve a problem in maths, the chances are that your plans cannot be brought to fruition.

Mattress

✚ **Lying comfortably on a mattress** – a warning not to get too comfortable in some situation; doing so might lead you into trouble.

♦ **Uncomfortable mattress** – denotes marital problems.

Maze *See* **Labyrinth**

Meadows
✖ ✚ Rich meadows full of flowers presage years of plenty, but contain a warning to lay up provisions for less prosperous times.
See also **Fields**

Meal *See* **Eating**

Meat *See* **Butcher, Food**

Medicine
♦ ✖ A sign that you will encounter some difficulty that you will, however, readily overcome.
See also **Doctor, Hospital, Illness, Nurse**

Medium
● If you attend a seance in your dream, in which a medium gets in touch with someone dear to you who is deceased, this most likely simply reflects the degree to which you miss the individual concerned and a fervent desire to be reunited.
See also **Ancestor, Death**

Melody
✖ Hearing a melody in your dream is generally a good omen, indicating that you will meet people. If the melody is familiar, you may meet with old friends.

Mending
♦ ● **Mending clothes** – you may be expressing resentment at something in your life which you feel is

'worn out'. Alternatively, it may express your desire to hang on to something cherished.

✖ **Mending fences** – your subconscious is pointing to the need to bring a quarrel to an end.

Menu

✖ An omen of a whole new series of opportunities that will present themselves to you. Try to remember whether the prices were within your range. This could be an omen of whether or not you finally opt to make a change in your lifestyle.

See also **Banquet, Food, Restaurant**

Mercy

✖ ♦ ● A dream of showing mercy to someone presages a life of harmony at home. Being shown mercy may be a subconscious admission that you have done something wrong, and a longing for forgiveness.

Meringue *See* **Food**

Mermaid

● **In a man's dream** – she symbolizes his ideal woman or a particular individual he would like to get to know but whom he feels will reject him.

♦ **In a woman's dream** – she represents a rival of some kind, most probably for a loved one's affections.

See also **Sea**

Merry-go-round

♦ ● Often a sign that in waking life, too, you feel you are going round in circles rather than making any definite progress. Riding a fairground horse also sometimes has strong sexual significance.

See also **Amusement park, Fairground, Riding**

Microscope

✚ ◆ ● Your subconscious is reminding you to consider the options that are before you particularly carefully. You may also feel that there are invisible barriers blocking your progress, and that you need to overcome them.
See also **Laboratory, Scientist**

Milk

● Milk can represent semen. If a man pours milk on a woman, this symbolizes the desire for sexual union. But dreams of milk may also be nostalgic yearning for the simplicity of the infant's life at its mother's breast.
See also **Drink**

Mill/miller

✖ ◆ An augur of wealth and happiness. If the dream is an unhappy one, it may be that in waking life you are feeling 'ground down'.

◆ **Being a miller** – denotes dissatisfaction with your own efficiency.

◆ ✖ **Someone else as a miller** – may indicate your critical feelings about a colleague or friend who is not hard working, or your admiration for one who is.

Millionaire

✖ An omen of forthcoming good fortune, whether or not in your dream all this wealth seems to buy happiness.
See also **Money**

Minaret

✖ To dream of a minaret is an omen of travel to foreign countries and adventures in exotic places.

Mine

✖ **Working in a mine** – an omen that you will gain wealth through your own labours.

✚ **Exploding mines** – a warning from your subconscious to be on guard in situations that could 'blow up in your face'.

Minstrels

✖ **Medieval minstrels** – presage interesting developments in your love life.
See also **Melody, Music**

Mirage

◆ Watching something apparently real fade away as you approach is a sign that you have taken on a hopeless task. The promises of a loved one or friend will probably turn out to be false.

Mire

◆ Being stuck in the mire – either on horseback, in a car, or on foot – points strongly to dissatisfaction with your life. You feel 'bogged down'.

Mirror

◆ A mirror usually refers to vanity and selfishness, but it can also mean a mask or the face with which the person greets the world.

✚ **To break a mirror** – a warning of bad luck.
See also **Faces**

Miscarriage

✚ ◆ If you are pregnant and dream of a miscarriage, this is not an omen as such. You are just a little nervous about the prospect of birth and motherhood as a whole.

If you are not pregnant, however, your subconscious could be warning you to take care over health problems. Alternatively, it may be a sign that you are worried about the possibility of a 'miscarriage' of justice.

See also **Baby, Birth**

Miser

◆ **Being a miser** – portends that you will not find wealth, owing to selfishness.

◆ **A friend as a miser** – whether you realize it or not, you harbour unflattering thoughts about that person's character.

Missionary

● **Being a missionary** – you are hoping, deep down, that you may have a chance to reorganize your life and lead an existence that is less materialistic.

◆ **Meeting missionaries** – your subconscious is warning you against being too easily influenced.

See also **God, Jesus**

Mistress *See* **Adultery**

Molasses *See* **Food**

Monastery/convent

● **Man enters a monastery/woman enters a convent** – you are simply anxious to have more time to yourself.

● **Woman enters a monastery** – you are likely to be anxious to free yourself of certain inhibitions.

● **Man enters a convent** – you would like to have more women friends who do not make sexual demands.

Money

A symbol of value and those things that are valuable, such as power, strength and sex. Dreams can be about lacking or losing money (for example, relationships, youth, abilities, business, etc.) or being confident about having money.

◆ **Stealing money** – the dreamer is trying to weaken someone.

◆ **Money being denied** – love being withheld.

◆ **Cheap goods** – poor behaviour.

See also **Accounts, Bank, Borrowing, Millionaire**

Monster

◆ **Being pursued** – bad fortune is ahead.

✖ **Killing a monster** – a successful outcome to problems.

Moon/moonlight

● You are likely to crave some element of romance in your life. For a woman, a dream of the moon may also act as a reminder that her menstrual period is due.

✖ ● **The moon growing full** – a dream reflecting on or wishing for a woman's pregnancy.

● **Travelling to the moon** – a dream of longing, either for great adventure or for something unattainable.

See also **Eclipse**

Moonstone

✖ Dreaming of these cloudy gemstones indicates some confusion or mystery in your life which, while puzzling, is not painful.

Mop

◆ **Using a mop** – a sign from your unconscious that you regret something said or done.

✚ **An old, dirty mop** – a warning not to believe or circulate rumours and gossip.

See also **Cleaning, Dirtiness, Washing**

Morgue

◆ **Yourself as a body in a morgue** – an indication that you are dreading some unpleasant task or event.

✚ **Finding a body in a morgue** – a warning to guard your health very carefully, especially if the person is known to you.

See also **Death**

Morning sickness

● For a woman to dream of this symptom of pregnancy may express her yearning for a baby. If she is pregnant, it may simply be a physiological dream.

Mortar

◆ ● **Mixing mortar** – a portent that all is not well at home or among your friends, and of your desire for people to 'stick together'.

Mortgage

● ✚ **Taking out a mortgage** – you may simply be keen to settle down. Alternatively, your subconscious could be warning you to make provision for the future.

◆ **Foreclosure** – usually reflects a genuine, waking concern.

See also **House, Money**

Moss
✖ **Lush green moss** – a happy domestic life and children.
◆ **Brown dry moss** – fears of barrenness and loneliness.

Moth *See* **Insect**

Mother
● If your mother figures in your dream, she may in fact be symbolic of some other aspect of your life: a need for comfort or love, perhaps. Take careful note of the dream sequence and your attitude towards your mother in the dream. If your mother is actually deceased, your dream of her may represent a death wish on your part – that you will meet again before too long.
See also **Family, Incest, Parents**

Mother-in-law
◆ Such a dream is frequently a reflection of a desire to flout authority.
See also **Family**

Motorcycle *See* **Journeys**

Mountains
✖ **The summit of a mountain** – a sign of ability, achievement, experience.
✚ **Difficulty in reaching the top** – don't waste your time on over-ambitious projects.
◆ **Falling down a mountain** – decline, perhaps in old age, is on the way.
See also **Climbing**

Mourning

✖ An omen of improved fortunes after a time of unhappiness.

See also **Bereavement, Death**

Mouth

✚ ◆ Your subconscious is trying to warn you of the merits of discretion. If teeth are visible, you may be subjected to unjust rumours by those you thought friends.

See also **Faces, Kiss, Lips, Teeth**

Muffins *See* **Baker/baking, Food**

Murder

◆ **Committing a murder** – you are no doubt feeling intense anger, either against a particular individual or the world at large.

◆ **Dreamer as the victim** – reflects a sense of being victimized in waking life, whether in a work or social context.

See also **Crime, Death**

Museum

◆ **Boring exhibits** – a sign of dissatisfaction with life.

✖ **Interesting exhibits** – a portent of a highly rewarding period ahead.

Music

✖ **Beautiful sounds** – an omen of future happiness.

◆ **Discordant sounds** – prospects are not so bright.

See also **Orchestra**

Musk *See* **Fragrance**

Mustard *See* **Food**

Mutiny

♦ ● **Taking part in a mutiny** – signifies repressed anger and the desire to escape some oppressive circumstance or person.

♦ ✚ **People mutinying against you** – a fearful dream expressing anxiety about losing your place, perhaps at work or in the family. It may contain a warning to re-evaluate things and change your ways.

Mutton *See* **Food**

Mystery

● A dream of a mystery story generally shows you are seeking after the true meaning of life and an understanding of the origins of the universe.
See also **Detective**

Nagging

♦ **Being nagged** – you may have left things undone and feel that you deserve nagging.

♦ **Doing the nagging** – may express anxiety that people don't like you.

Nails

✖ ● If you hammer in nails in your dream, it means you will work hard and honourably. Alternatively, you could be expressing a desire to be violent.

♦ **Problems hammering in a nail** – in a man, reflects buried anxieties about sexual potency. In a woman, may mean she has a secret abhorrence of sex.

Nakedness *See* **Nudity**

Name

● **Changing your name** – you would like to change a major aspect of your lifestyle.

● **Forgetting your name** – you would like to eradicate some past action completely.

See also **Signature**

Napkins

⌘ **Wiping mouth or hands with a napkin** – you feel confident that you have completed some task satisfactorily.

● **Folded napkins** – you may be hoping for friendship from an admired colleague or acquaintance.

Napoleon

● The great French emperor is likely to symbolize the dreamer's father or some other authority figure or hero. You may be feeling in need of guidance or fatherly advice.

Napping *See* **Sleep/sleeping**

Nasturtiums *See* **Flowers**

Navigating

⌘ **Navigating through hazards** – expresses your determination to win despite the difficulties life puts in your way.

See also **Map**

Neighbours

● If, in waking life, you have little contact with them, it could be that they symbolize, in your dream, a desire to understand your own psychological make-up better, or simply that you would like to get to know them better.

Necklaces
✖ **A woman receiving one** – portends that she will have a happy marriage.

♦ **Losing one** – you may feel fearful of losing your loved one prematurely.

See also **Jewellery**

Nests
● **Birds making nests** – a fairly clear message about wanting marriage and family.

♦ ● **Destroying nests** – a dream showing aggression and the desire to break out of family ties.

✖ **Eggs in a nest** – coming into money.

♦ **Broken eggs in a nest** – points to problems in the family.

News/newspapers
✖ **Good news** – favourable times are due.

♦ **Bad news** – you will be distressed.

● **Newspapers** – You are probably hoping for novelty and surprise to enter your life.

Night
● ♦ It is possible that a dream set at night could refer to the dreamer's desire to ignore or hide problems. But a more straightforward interpretation could be that night is a background for many events that take place in dreams.

Nightmare
✚ ♦ This is an expression of very strong feelings of

conflict. Often a guilty secret is involved – perhaps of a
sexual nature – one that is not recognized. It is a
warning to admit the existence of the conflict.

Nose

✛ **Blocked-up** – your subconscious is warning you to
clear up matters that have been hanging over you for
some time.

◆ **Broken nose** – an omen of family problems.

● **Long nose** – generally has sexual connotations.

See also **Faces**

Nosedive

◆ Going into a nosedive while flying an aeroplane is
an omen of a wild romantic and sexual adventure,
probably one with a disastrous outcome. Alternatively,
it may express your fears that life is going out of
control.

Nudity

◆ ✛ Dreams of revealing all contain a message from
the subconscious that you should try being more open
about matters that have been bothering you. The dream
may also reflect a rebellious streak in you, one which
refuses to play the roles others cast you in, and contain
a warning about where such an attitude may lead.
Naturally there is also a sexual component to dreams of
nudity.

◆ **Being nude in an inappropriate setting** – for
instance, on a bus or at work, expresses fears that
people can 'see through you' and will reject you if you
do not keep up the facade you put on.

Numbers

In dreams if numbers are significant, they may relate to things or people other than the ones that appear in the dream and make interpretation difficult. More straightforwardly, they could be a reference to some business worry. Some numbers are important to certain people, and this may be reflected in a dream. Even numbers are associated with the feminine, odd with the male or the peculiar.

✖ ♦ **One** – stands for masculinity and probably sex, for isolation, unity or the sense that the dreamer is 'number one'.

✖ ♦ **Two** – means the two sides or two halves of anything, a pair.

✖ ♦ **Three** – signifies father, mother and child.

♦ **Three and four together** – may mean that one of the four functions of the mind – intellect opposed by emotion, and sensation opposed by intuition – is neglected.

✖ **Four** – unity and order, since the four functions are together and the being is whole.

● ✖ **Five** – always an important number, five refers to the five appendages of the body, also the fingers of the hands, and therefore indicates the life force.

● ✖ ♦ **Six** – may mean sex.

✖ **Seven** – traditionally this is a sacred number in Christianity and Judaism.

✖ **Nine** – perhaps relates to pregnancy and achievement.

✖ ♦ **Ten** – very often refers to the masculine and the feminine and therefore to marriage.

✖ ◆ **Twelve** – because twelve is used in the clock and the calendar, it may represent time.

Nurse
● Such a dream usually reflects a need for greater attention and assistance with some pressing problems.
See also **Accident, Hospital, Illness**

Nuts
✖ ✚ If nuts figure in your dream, the omens are usually excellent. However, nuts also mean male sexuality, and the dream may be a warning about problems in a relationship.
✖ **Cracking nuts** – you will find a way out of a difficult problem.

Nymph
✖ **Scantily clad nymph** – a wish-fulfilment dream.

Oar
◆ **Propelling a boat with oars** – you may feel that you are carrying a burden others should be sharing.
✖ **Oar breaking** – you may get into trouble soon, but it is within your powers to extricate yourself.

Obesity
✚ To dream of being overweight probably means that you should watch your diet – you may be too thin rather than too fat.
See also **Weight**

Objects
Many objects in dreams are thrown up by the unconscious to symbolize states of inner feeling. For

this reason many objects seem to have a near universal meaning. Interpretation depends on choosing the most likely explanation.

✖ ◆ **Long or pointed objects** – most frequently refer to the phallus, for example, a lighthouse, pen, hose or syringe.

✖ ◆ **Round or hollow objects** – representative of the female or feminine, especially if associated with women's traditional occupations, such as cooking.

Obligations

◆ ✖ **Yourself under an obligation** – you may be troubled by some responsibility. If you meet the responsibility in the dream it expresses confidence that your troubles will be short-lived.

◆ **Someone obliged to you** – you may be resenting favours done for others but never reciprocated.

Obstacles

◆ Objects seen in the dream as obstacles usually denote either difficulty, a sense of guilt or something else holding back the dreamer from realizing an ambition. It may be that the obstacle has deliberately been put in the way by the dreamer so that some problem need not be faced.

Ocean *See* Sea, Water

Odours

✖ **Pleasant scents** – an omen of good fortune.

◆ **Foul aroma** – does not augur favourably.

See also **Fragrance**

Ogre

◆ There is clearly some situation in your life that is proving overwhelming, even terrifying.
See also **Giant**

Oil

◆ ✖ Can mean slyness, wealth, sex.
✖ **Oiling machinery** – denotes a wish to introduce harmony among family and friends who may have fallen out.

Oil paintings *See* **Painting**

Old man or woman

◆ ✖ For elderly people to figure in a dream probably foretells burdens and cares, unless they are calm and wise. However, to dream of being an old maid is a sign that you will marry a fiery black-eyed musician!

Olives *See* **Food**

Onions *See* **Food**

Opals

✖ The blue-green gemstones presage prosperity and popularity when they appear in your dreams.
✚ **Losing opals** – you should be cautious in throwing your happiness away.

Opera *See* **Music, Singing, Stage, Theatre**

Operation

● You would like to rid yourself of an unsatisfactory relationship or other disappointing aspect of your life.
See also **Amputation, Doctor, Hospital, Nurse, Surgeon**

Opium *See* **Drugs**

Opposites
Dreams often illustrate some idea, conflict, wish or
emotion, which is translated into a symbol, by its
opposite, for example dark/light, hot/cold, sweet/sour.
The interpreter will have to work hard to understand
what the unconscious is really saying. But these
opposites usually refer to basic attitudes, feelings and
characteristics.

Oracle
● If you consult an oracle in your dreams, you may
find that the opposite of his or her predictions actually
occurs. Such dreams may also reflect a hidden need for
guidance and advice.

Oranges *See* **Food**

Orchestra
● **Conducting** – you would like to be in a position of
power.
◆ **Unable to follow the score** – symbolizes a failure to
cope with some other area of life entirely.
✖ **Jazz orchestra** – presages carefree times in good
company.
See also **Music**

Organ music
◆ **Thunderous organ music** – denotes some religious
feeling of guilt.
◆ **Electric organ** – you may suspect the player of
being not quite genuine.
See also **Music**

Orgy
✖ Your subconscious is trying to encourage you to take a more relaxed approach to a sexual relationship.

Orphan
✚ Your subconscious is warning you that you lack a sense of purpose in life.
See also **Death, Parents**

Ostrich *See* **Birds**

Oven
● ✖ ◆ The symbol for the womb. Therefore it could mean a wish for a child, or the fear of having a child. A straightforward explanation is that it stands for housekeeping, eating and cooking.
See also **Baker/baking, Cooking, Kitchen**

Owl *See* **Birds**

Packing
If you are packing up or packing away, it may be that you are trying to get too many, or too few, activities into your day.
See also **Luggage**

Paddlewheel
✖ ✚ If you dream that you are on a boat with a paddlewheel, it is an omen that you will travel, though the dream contains a warning to guard against recklessness on your voyage.
See also **Journeys, Ship**

Padlock
◆ **Unable to open a padlock** – a dream presaging frustration and discontent.

✚ **Opening a padlock** – beware prying into the business of others.
See also **Key, Lock**

Pages
● ✄ **Turning pages in books or magazines** – may point to an unconscious desire to improve your knowledge of things. Predictively, the message is of future prosperity.
See also **Book, Reading**

Pagoda
● If a pagoda appears in your dream, it indicates a wish to expand your horizons, perhaps by taking up a new interest.

Pain
✚ Your subconscious is warning you about taking particular care of your physical and emotional health.
See also **Accident, Doctor, Drugs, Hospital, Illness**

Painting
◆ **House painting** – perhaps you have something to hide, or maybe your health requires care. If someone else is painting the house, you may be harbouring a suspicion about that person's sincerity.
● **Oil paintings** – As symbols of wealth and prestige, oil paintings in dreams are a wish for material success and the recognition of one's achievements.
● **Picture painting** – may symbolize the desire to be more creative.

Palace
✄ Usually means success.
See also **Castles, Royalty**

Palm-reading

● **Having your palm read** – a sign that you are feeling worried about the future and are seeking reassurance and clues as to how things will unfold.

◆ **Reading another's palm** – may be an expression of concern for their future well-being, or you may feel that you know something concerning their future that they don't.

See also **Fortune-telling**

Pan

✖ Greek god of fields. To dream of Pan, the goat-footed deity is an omen of good humour helping to overcome adversity.

Panic

✚ A dream, in which panic is the key emotion, is a sign that you should beware of losing your temper in the near future.

Pantry

✖ If you dream of a pantry stocked with good food, it portends future happiness and security, although it may also be your subconscious compensating for present hardships.

◆ ✚ **Empty pantry** – may reflect on your present circumstances, or be a warning of future difficulties and loneliness.

Paradise

✖ This is an entirely happy omen for your future and friendships.

Paralysis
◆ Dreams of paralysis refer to your state of mind rather than a physical condition.
See also **Accident, Illness**

Parcel
✖ **Delivered to dreamer** – signifies good things to come.
◆ **Carrying a parcel** – the dreamer will have to do something unpleasant.

Parchment
✚ Dreams featuring an old parchment document carry a message from your subconscious to re-examine some aspect of your past.

Parents
✖ A dream of both your parents usually symbolizes something else completely, rather than reflecting your relationship with them. Indeed, they generally represent the male and female sides of the personality.
See also **Adoption, Family, Father, Mother**

Paris
● **Visiting Paris** – may be inspired by memories of an actual visit to the city, or express a yearning for something exotic and romantic to happen.

Park
● ✖ To dream of a park means either that you want to be more relaxed or that you are happy to have the time to enjoy more leisure.

Parliament
✖ Dreams of standing for parliament are an omen of

greater responsibilities that will arise in some other area of life.

Parsley *See* Food

Party
♦ **Giving a party** – an indication that your popularity has been waning of late.
✖ **Going to a party** – an omen of busy times ahead.

Passport
✚ If you dream that your passport has expired, this is a message from your subconscious that it is your image that needs updating.
See also Travel

Patent
✚ **Patent leather shoes** – if your shiny black shoes are pinching your feet, it is a warning to avoid situations a spouse might not understand.
♦ **Taking out a patent** – dreaming of taking out a patent on an invention expresses anxiety about others stealing credit due to you.

Path
♦ **Narrow and rough** – a difficult time ahead.
♦ **Trying to find the path** – you may not be able to achieve what you want.
✖ **Green and pleasant** – you have freedom of activity.

Patio
● ♦ If your house has a patio, this points to a wish for more quiet times in the garden. If you do not own one, it indicates social ambition and dissatisfaction with your present standing.

Pauper
✚ **Becoming a pauper** – contains a warning to curb your selfish inclination before you lose friends.
See also **Beggar, Poverty**

Paw
✖ In dreams, a dog or other pet giving you its paw presages new friendships from unlikely places.
◆ A woman who dreams of paws may be suffering the unwelcome attentions of a man, who wishes to 'paw' her.
See also **Animals**

Pawnbroker
✖ A sign that you will succeed in rising above current problems.
See also **Gold, Money**

Peacock *See* **Birds**

Pearl
◆ ✖ In dreams pearls often symbolize the whole person, or a rounded life. Losing a pearl would therefore represent a serious upset or loss, while finding one would presage a new sense of peace and harmony.
See also **Jewellery**

Pension
✚ Your subconscious is warning you to make careful provision for the future.
See also **Retirement**

Perfume *See* **Fragrance, Odours**

Phantoms *See* **Ghosts**

Piano
✖ **Playing well** – augurs well for the future.
◆ **Playing out of tune** – you are anxious that your
skills are not really adequate for a new appointment
you are about to take up.
See also **Music**

Poison
✚ Sometimes a warning from the subconscious of
incipient poor health.
See also **Illness**

Poker *See* **Gambling**

Police
● Not necessarily a sign of guilt but of a desire for
greater security.
See also **Crime**

Portrait
✚ Your subconscious is pointing out that you need to
take more care over your appearance.

Poverty
◆ **If desperate** – a very unlucky omen.
✚ **Help given to the poor** – calls will be made on your
generosity.
See also **Beggar, Pauper**

Prayer
● Analysis of a dream involving prayer must
inevitably take into account what the dreamer was
asking for. However, such a dream probably indicates
that, at present, something the dreamer has been

striving for seems beyond his or her reach.
See also **Church, God, Jesus**

Priest *See* **Clergy**

Prince/princess *See* **Royalty**

Prison
♦ You may well have a guilty secret, but it is equally possible that your dream is symbolizing a feeling of isolation that you have in waking life.
See also **Cell, Jail, Quarantine**

Prize
✘ You will most likely find recognition at work.

Proposal
● ✘ If a woman receives a proposal in her dream, this could well be an example of wish-fulfilment. However, the proposal could also symbolize the prospect of a job offer.
See also **Engagement, Marriage, Wedding**

Prostitute
✚ **In a man's dream** – sometimes not entirely what it seems, for his subconscious could in fact be warning him against some sort of deal that he has been offered on a plate but that could have serious consequences.
● **In a woman's dream** – she would like to be more sexually adventurous in waking life.

Pulling
♦ This signifies attraction. Consider if perhaps it may be towards the wrong people or things.

Punishment

♦ The conscience is trying to punish some wrong-doing.

Puppet

♦ This is precisely how you feel in waking life – manipulated and completely under someone else's control.
See also **Doll, Ventriloquist**

Purse

♦ A symbol of loss of femininity, and the approach of the menopause.
See also **Money**

Pushing

♦ Perhaps you feel someone, or an event, is making you do something you don't want to do.

Puzzle

♦ ⌘ Trying to solve a puzzle in a dream is an omen that complications will arise but that, with attention, they will soon be solved.

Pygmy *See* **Dwarf**

Pyramid

♦ You are anxious about the possibility of a love triangle.

Quarantine

♦ You are feeling isolated in waking life, too, for some reason, though not necessarily through your own doing.
See also **Illness, Prison**

Quarrel *See* **Argument**

Queen *See* **Royalty**

Queue

◆ The chances are that life has been very routine of late and so far you have failed to achieve a goal you have set.
See also **Shopping**

Quicksand

◆ You are anxious about being drawn into something that you would rather steer clear of.
See also **Accident, Falling**

Rabbi *See* **Clergy**

Race

◆ ✖ To dream of a race means that you have a rival. If you win while gambling at a race, the omens are good.
See also **Running**

Radio

◆ You are currently anxious about a lack of communication between yourself and a loved one or colleague.
See also **Television**

Rage

✚ Your subconscious is warning you about the dangers of losing self-control.
See also **Aggression, Argument**

Rain

✖ You will soon have more energy for all your activities.

Rainbow

✖ You should regard this as a very optimistic sign for the future, just as it was when it appeared in the biblical account of the Great Flood.

Ranch *See* Farm, Farmer

Rape

◆ **In a woman's dream** – she fears being taken advantage of, not only sexually but in some other area of life.

◆ **In a man's dream** – he has perhaps been repressing certain violent aspects of his character and may need to seek professional guidance.

Razor

◆ **In a man's dream** – shaving is often a sign that he has been failing to assert himself of late.

◆ **Cutting self** – indicative of financial problems ahead.

◆ **In a woman's dream** – she is anxious about being belittled and not valued at all.

See also **Barber, Blood, Hair**

Reading

Try to recall as carefully as you can what you were reading in your dream and, if it was a book, its title and subject matter. These details should help to provide valuable clues as to the meaning of your dream.

See also **Book, Illiteracy, Letter, Library**

Reception *See* Party

Redundancy *See* Dismissal

Refugees

◆ You have been thinking about freeing yourself from an entanglement or bad relationship in waking life, as well as possibly changing your job.
See also **Exile**

Religion *See* **Church, Clergy, God, Jesus**

Rescue

● You would like to change certain aspects of your emotional life.

Resolutions

✢ Your subconscious is advising you that it would indeed be wise to make certain changes.

Restaurant

◆ Your subconscious is telling you that you have been rather hard on yourself recently.

◆ **Having lunch in a restaurant** – augurs ill for your progress at work, but it may just be a physiological dream arising out of hunger pangs.
See also **Food, Menu**

Retirement

✢ You may have to work harder.
See also **Pension**

Revenge

◆ **Dreamer takes revenge** – this may indicate that you should try to be kinder.

✢ **Revenge taken on dreamer** – beware of some of the people around you.

Revolution
◆ Perhaps you should think of change.
See also **War**

Reward *See* **Prize**

Riddle
◆ May indicate an old relationship that needs some new life if it is to go on for a long time. Otherwise it might mean general confusion.

Riding
◆ **Jumping fences** – your subconscious is reminding you about certain obstacles you are up against in waking life.
● **Galloping** – frequently of sexual significance.
See also **Animals, Merry-go-round**

Ring
● Symbolic of a desire to form some lasting attachment. It could well be a romantic liaison but there is a possibility, too, that such a dream may actually relate to some sort of contract or business agreement.

Riot
✚ ◆ A dream of rioting is always disturbing and foretells a likely disaster.

Rival *See* **Jealousy, Race**

River
◆ **Murky water** – someone is having an undesirable influence over your emotions.
✖ **Clear water** – good fortune lies ahead.
See also **Flood, Sea, Water**

Road
✘ **Straight road** – an omen of success.
◆ **Winding road** – life's complexities are proving too much right now.
See also **Alley, Journeys**

Robbery
✚ Your subconscious is probably warning you against taking notice of others who may well be interfering in your private affairs.
See also **Burglary, Crime, Money**

Rocket
● Most frequently relates to unfulfilled sexual desires.

Rocks
◆ These are obstacles to be surmounted in your life.

Room
✘ A room in general stands for feminine qualities and home.
See also **Door**

Roots
● ✘ ◆ Basic, life-giving and entangling qualities are involved in your situation. These qualities should give you clues about the interpretation.

Rope
◆ **Dreamer is tied up** – represents how you feel in waking life: restricted and unable to act freely for whatever reason.
◆ **Dreamer ties someone up** – you are fearful of losing the affections of a loved one.
See also **Abduction**

Royalty

✚ ● **King** – If you dream of an embarrassing meeting with a monarch, your subconscious is warning you against ideas above your station. If you dream of being a king, you have an unconscious wish for greater authority and respect; you believe you are worth more than others seem to believe. Someone else as king may represent your father or some other powerful figure from childhood; you may wish for help and guidance from that person.

● **Prince** – you seek confirmation of your sex appeal.

◆ **Princess** – you feel guilty deep down about having been too demanding of others.

● **Queen** – if you dream of the Queen coming to tea, you are among very many thousands who regularly experience this dream theme and for whom it is likely to be a sign that they feel overlooked and would appreciate more attention.

Rudeness

✚ **Dreamer is rude** – you should watch out that you may have to answer to someone in authority over you.

✚ **Others are rude to dreamer** – may be a warning about bad temper.

Ruins

◆ ✖ These mean broken contracts, appointments, engagements. Ancient ruins signify travel.

Running

● **Away from something** – you would like to escape from some unpleasant or threatening situation.

● **Towards something** – reflects certain burning ambitions yet to be achieved.
See also **Escape, Exhaustion, Fugitive, Race**

Sacrifice

♦ **Offering a sacrifice** – a sign that you need to assuage some element of guilt.
♦ **Dreamer as a sacrificial offering** – you feel resentful against others who seem to have been taking advantage of you.
See also **God**

Safe

♦ **Dreamt by a man** – he fears that a guilty secret may eventually be discovered.
♦ **Dreamt by a woman** – she is harbouring fears about her sexuality and may even be anxious about the fact that she has still to lose her virginity.
See also **Gold, Money**

Saint

♦ ✖ **Meeting a saint** – consider carefully the possible significance of his or her patronage.
♦ **Martyrdom** – symbolic of your own life being somewhat under pressure.

Salary

♦ **Lower pay than usual** – you have probably been overspending.
♦ **Higher pay than usual** – you have not been as straightforward as you might have been recently.
✖ **Salary increase** – an omen of some sort of surprise, but one not necessarily connected with your job.
See also **Money**

Salt
◆ ✖ Salt in a dream usually means difficulties and discord. However, it can signify the essential soul of the dreamer.

Sand
● ✖ ◆ This can mean time, and how much you feel you have left to do all that you want. Alternatively, to dream of sand could straightforwardly mean that you would like a holiday.
See also **Beach, Sea**

Satan *See* Devil

Savage
◆ There may be some wilder aspect to your personality that has been struggling hard to get out but that you have been keeping under control.
See also **Cannibals**

Scaffold *See* Hanging

Scales
◆ If you dream of something being weighed, this symbolizes the fact that you are, in waking life, trying to weigh up the pros and cons of some decision you have to make. Alternatively, the dream could represent justice that you are seeking.
See also **Judge, Jury**

Scandal
◆ The chances are that your conscience has been bothering you.

School

♦ Sometimes even those in middle age dream of attending school as an adult and, while dreaming, are aware that they are far too old to be there. It is frequently a sign of lack of confidence and a fear of not being entirely *au fait* with one's work.
See also **Kindergarten**

Scientist

⌘ ♦ Your subconscious may be trying to encourage you to investigate new possibilities as far as work, lifestyle or even holidays are concerned. It may also be a sign that you should try to think through a current problem rather more logically than you have been, putting problems to the side for the moment.
♦ **Dreamer as astronomer** – you are feeling very much on the outside of things and in need of someone who can share your life and endeavours.
See also **Laboratory, Microscope**

Scissors

♦ You either fear castration or feel rather 'cut off' from the rest of society.

Scolding

♦ **Being scolded** – you are probably in danger of being too sure of yourself.
● **Scolding** – you would like to feel superior.

Scratch

✚ **Dreamer scratching others** – beware of being bad tempered.
✚ **Dreamer being scratched** – a warning that someone is planning you harm.

Screaming

◆ Most usually a clear sign of a cry for help.
Remember, too, that even if someone else is screaming
in your dream, this 'someone else' could be
representing a particular aspect of your personality.

Sea

● ✚ If the sea is empty, take warning that you may be
for a time lacking in relationships. If you dream of the
seaside, you may feel you are missing out on pleasure.
See also **Anchor, Ship, Water**

Seance *See* Medium

Searching

◆ The dreamer is looking for some fulfilment,
although he or she may know what it is and be
unwilling to admit it because of the consequences.
Perhaps the search is for identity.
See also **Hunting**

Seasons

✖ **Spring** – the happiness of childhood.
✖ **Summer** – the spirit of youth.
✖ **Autumn** – maturity and wisdom.
◆ **Winter** – old age and degeneration.

Secret

◆ If you hear a secret in a dream, this means someone
you have trusted will let you down.

Senses

These are equated with the four elements of the mind.
Sight means the intellect; hearing, its opposite, the

emotions. Smell indicates intuition; taste/touch, its opposite, sensation.

Servant *See* **Maid**

Sewing

✖ Harmony and peace will reign at home.

Sexuality

There are a great many dream symbols that are believed to relate to sexuality: everything from horse-riding to snakes and flying.

● **Sex change** – may have a different interpretation altogether: a desire to switch one's job, for instance.
See also **Eunuch, Impotence, Intercourse**

Shadows

◆ You will need to consider whether this signifies that you are being outshone by someone else. It may also represent some tragic event that has darkened your world for the present.

Shame

◆ To suffer shameful feelings in a dream may mean you are doubtful about your ability to cope with more responsibility.

Shaving *See* **Razor**

Ship

✖ **Calm voyage** – represents forging ahead with one's plans.
◆ **Stormy voyage** – an omen of emotional upset.
See also **Journeys, Sea, Yacht**

Shoes

♦ ● In general, dreams about shoes either reflect that one is having trouble with one's feet or a fervent desire for greater freedom.
See also **Barefoot, Feet**

Shooting *See* **Weapons**

Shopping

✖ A sign that you will have to reach a major decision in life quite soon.
See also **Clothes, Market**

Siblings

♦ Dream about an argument with a brother or sister and you are probably feeling somewhat emotionally insecure.
See also **Family, Incest**

Signature

● Often signifies a searching for one's true identity. It is, incidentally, a fairly common dream among newly married women who are getting used to a new surname.
See also **Forgery, Name**

Silk

✖ Fabrics made of silk denote high ambition that is satisfied. Old silk indicates a pride in ancestors.

Silver

♦ Dreaming of silver may mean you are too dependent on money at the expense of contentment with more basic things. This may bring anxiety.

Singing
In order to interpret this dream, you will need to recall the title of the song you were singing or listening to.
♦ **Singing out of tune** – an omen of troublesome times ahead.
See also **Music**

Sister *See* **Family, Siblings**

Skeleton/skull
♦ Your subconscious is trying to remind you that you need to know someone a little better before you make a judgment about him or her because appearances can be deceptive. Such a dream may also reflect a fear of death.

Sky
✖ ♦ Signifies the heavens, boundless space and perhaps avoidance of problems. Or it may relate to creativity that needs to be encouraged.

Sleep/sleeping
♦ The dream may have an obvious meaning, such as that you need more sleep, or it may indicate that some part of the emotions is dead/asleep.

✖ **Napping** – dreams of taking naps during the day signify feelings of ease and plenty, and are an omen of financial security.

Smoke
♦ A signal from your subconscious that plans you have been making could be fraught with danger.
See also **Fire**

Smoking
● Dream of smoking where it is prohibited and this could well be a sign that you would dearly like to break with convention, even at the risk of the world branding you an eccentric.

Smuggling
◆ There is likely to be some guilty secret that you share and that you fear the other party might accidentally reveal.
See also **Crime**

Snakes *See* **Animals**

Snow
◆ The emotions are cold, either those of the dreamer or of someone else.
✤ **Clean snow** – signifies innocence.
◆ **Dirty snow** – implies guilt.
See also **Ice**

Soldiers
✤ ◆ May refer to self-control or to discipline from outside, or perhaps a desire for a heroic life.
See also **Army**

Spade
◆ There is hard work to be done.

Spectacles
✚ ✤ If you normally do not use them, your subconscious could be warning you to examine your future prospects more carefully than you have up to now. Alternatively, it could mean a happy family and that you are coping well with obligations.

Speech
◆ There is something you feel very strongly about but are far too reserved to discuss openly in waking life.

Sports *See* Games

Stage
You will need to consider the part you were playing if you dream of appearing on stage, in order to understand the underlying significance of this symbolism.
◆ **Forgotten lines** – almost certainly suggests a lack of confidence in waking life.
See also **Actor/actress, Applause, Fame, Theatre**

Stain *See* Dirtiness

Stairs
✘ **Climbing stairs** – signifies the achievement of ambition.
◆ **Falling downstairs** – you have doubts about former aspirations.
See also **Escalator, Falling**

Stars
● A sign that you are striving to achieve some important personal goal.
See also **Scientist, Sky**

Starvation
◆ Dreams of food relate to the emotions. Thus, a dream of starvation is indicative of emotional deprivation and a feeling that you are destined to cope alone.
See also **Food**

Stealing

◆ **Dreamer steals** – it will be necessary to look at the motives of some of your actions.

✚ **Dreamer accused of stealing** – beware the misunderstanding of friends.

See also **Burglary, Crime, Robbery**

Stilts

● You have been feeling somewhat insignificant of late and are making a plea to the world to take more notice of you.

Stock exchange

✖ **Making a profit on shares** – an omen of happiness.

◆ **Making a loss on shares** – you are fearful that a once meaningful relationship is close to its end.

See also **Gambling, Money**

Stone

◆ Indicates concern about a lack of feeling if people or live animals are turned to stone.

Stork *See* **Birds**

Storm

◆ You can expect a stormy scene or argument with a loved one.

See also **Lightning**

Stranger

◆ A male stranger who figures in a big way in a dream indicates the hidden part of the personality.

Strike

● ◆ Dream of going on strike, and the chances are

that either you would like to draw some aspect of your life to a conclusion or that you bear an unspoken grudge.

Subway
♣ ♦ Your subconscious is advising you, by using a symbolic direct route, to get straight to the point in negotiations you are conducting.

Success
♦ Probably an attempt to compensate for a sense of failure.

Suicide
♣ ♦ Far from being an omen of your own impending death, such a dream is a sign that you should change direction in life.
See also **Death**

Sun
♣ **Sunbathing** – usually an omen of fulfilment and happiness.
♣ **Getting sunburnt** – be wary of anyone who is excessively charming on a first meeting.
See also **Eclipse**

Surgeon
♦ You may have the feeling that someone is interfering with your life.
See also **Hospital, Operation**

Swan *See* **Birds**

Swimming

⌘ **Winning a race** – you will soon achieve remarkable success.

♦ **Out of your depth** – this is almost certainly how you feel in waking life at work or within a current relationship.

See also **Drowning, Water**

Table *See* **Furniture**

Taxes

⌘ You feel a debt towards someone for the help that has been given to you.

See also **Money**

Teacher

⌘ ● ♦ **Dreamer as teacher** – he or she is willing to help others learn. Alternatively, it could mean a desire to have more authority or a fear of using such authority.

⌘ ♦ **Others as teachers** – they could be able to help the dreamer, or the dreamer might be afraid of being judged for some action or of being regarded as inferior.

See also **School**

Tears

♦ If you dream of being in tears, it is likely that some small disaster will occur. If others cry, your unhappiness may affect other people.

Teasing

♦ ⌘ May be a reaction to unsatisfactory relationships. But it might also mean you are a cheerful and popular person.

Teeth

✚ ♦ It is exceedingly common to dream of losing a tooth, or even of all one's teeth falling out. Such a dream may well occur simply because you grind or gnash your teeth in your sleep. But the dream may also be a reminder from your subconscious that it is time to make an appointment with the dentist. It can also be an omen of financial problems.

Telephone

✚ Sometimes a sign that someone is anxious to contact you but is hesitating to do so in case you would not welcome communication. Alternatively, your subconscious may be reminding *you* to contact someone else.

Television

✖ ♦ Your subconscious is advising you not to be too much of a spectator in life but to be more participatory, living it to the full.
See also **Radio**

Temper *See* **Argument, Rage**

Terror *See* **Fear**

Theatre

● You would dearly like to be the centre of attention for once.
See also **Actor/actress, Applause, Stage**

Thirst

● If you are thirsty in your dream, this may actually be

the case in waking life. However, your subconscious may be resorting to use of a pun, thereby showing that you are 'thirsting after' something or someone.
See also **Alcohol, Drink**

Throne *See* **Royalty**

Thunder *See* **Storm**

Tide

✖ **Incoming tide** – may mean you will soon be better off.

◆ **Outgoing tide** – you will have something more to worry about.

See also **Beach, Sea**

Tie

● **In a woman's dream** – if she buys a man a tie, she is symbolically entering into a physical relationship with him.

◆ **In a man's dream** – if he has problems in fixing his tie, this relates to fears of impotence.

Time

● ✖ ◆ **A day** – a symbol for a life.
✖ **The morning** – means youth.
✖ **The afternoon** – signifies maturity.
✖ ◆ **The evening** – the close of life.
See also **Clock**

Tower

◆ If you dream of a tower in the distance, you may be wasting your time in a relationship.

Toys
✚ **Buying toys** – your subconscious is warning you against frivolity.
● **Playing with toys** – you would like more free time for relaxation.
See also **Child/children, Doll**

Traffic jam
◆ You feel that you have reached an impasse in waking life, and are failing to make progress.
See also **Journeys**

Train *See* **Journeys**

Tramp
● You would dearly like to shed the chains of convention and responsibility and, as it were, be your own person for a change.

Transformation
If something is changed into another thing, the two are connected and may be opposites in the dreamer, two sides to his or her nature.
◆ **Dreamer becoming a beast** – shows an awareness that some of the dreamer's behaviour is unacceptable.
● ◆ **The beautiful becoming ugly** – stands for the conflict between desire and inhibition.

Travel
● ✖ You may be searching for new fields and excitements. Take note of the surroundings: they will give you a more precise clue about your feelings.
See also **Accent, Journeys**

Treasure
✖ An omen that you will finally succeed after sustained effort.
See also **Gold, Money, Prize**

Tree
● There is frequently a spiritual significance, indicating a desire for knowledge and a seeking after truth.
◆ **Cutting down fir trees** – you may be harbouring fears of impending disaster.
✖ **Walking through fir trees** – signifies good fortune and happiness.
See also **Forest, Foliage, Fungus, Jungle**

Triangle
✖ This is a good omen and may refer to the Christian Trinity, the three aspects of the individual – being, consciousness and love – or the spiritual side of the dreamer.
See also **Pyramid**

Trumpet
✖ Those who dream of blowing a trumpet will be surprised by some unexpected success.
See also **Music**

Tunnel *See* **Journeys, Subway**

Twins/triplets
◆ **Having a multiple birth** – may have nothing to do with pregnancy as such, but relate instead to two (or more) distinct parts of your personality that are in conflict.

♦ ✖ **Colleague or friend as your twin** – an indication that you have discovered an entirely surprising side to that person's nature.
See also **Baby, Birth, Child/Children, Siblings**

Ugliness
♦ A depressing outcome of a relationship.

Ukulele
● Hearing or seeing this instrument being played in a dream may be drawing your attention to something in the past, when life seemed simpler and more enjoyable.
● **Playing a ukulele** – a dream of escape into an easier life.
See also **Music**

Umbrella
♦ Your subconscious is telling you to take certain steps to ensure you are safe not only from the elements as such but from confidence tricksters or thieves.

Undressing
♦ A sign that you fear someone will discover something about you that you would rather remained a secret.
See also **Nudity**

Uniform
● You would like to be accepted as part of a group, whereas you feel very much an outsider on the whole.

University
✖ Your subconscious is reminding you that your rewards will come eventually through sustained effort.
See also **Examination, School**

Upholstery

✖ **Luxurious upholstery** – denotes your satisfaction
with your domestic arrangements.

◆ **Worn-out upholstery** – may be an early sign that
things at home need to change.
See also **Furniture**

Urn

✖ ◆ **Funeral urn** – the portent is of travel to
unknown places. If the urn contains the ashes of
someone known to you, you may be regretting a failed
friendship or estrangement.

Vampire

◆ An unpleasant symbol which probably relates to
your negative and destructive side.

Vegetables

◆ May refer to a feeling that your life is dull.
According to an old dream guide, 'Withered or decayed
vegetables bring unmitigated woe and sadness.'
See also **Food**

Veil

◆ There is something you want to hide.

Ventriloquist

◆ ✚ This is again very much how you feel in waking
life: like an automaton and in need of a change of
routine. It may also be a warning dream, indicating that
you should be more careful about what you say and to
whom.
See also **Puppet**

Vertigo
♦ A sign that you inwardly fear that life's everyday problems could well end up in a turmoil.
See also **Falling**

Victim
♦ **Dreamer as victim** – you probably feel that you are misunderstood and have enemies.
♦ **Others as victims** – you may feel you are undeservedly successful.

Vine/vineyard
✖ An omen for good fortune.

Violence *See* **Aggression, Fight, Murder, Rape, War**

Violin
● **Serenade** – usually indicates a desire for romance in one's life.
♦ **Playing untunefully** – an inner fear that you will never achieve your ambitions.
See also **Music, Orchestra**

Virgin Mary
✖ Usually a sign of forthcoming happiness. At times, too, she is the archetypal dream symbol of motherhood.

Volcano
✚ If an eruption is taking place, the dream is a warning that there is serious inner turmoil which needs to be examined. Lava pouring over a landscape is a warning that illness may be impending.

Vomiting

● You wish to rid yourself of certain unpleasant factors in your life.
See also **Illness**

Voting *See* **Election**

Voyage *See* **Journeys, Sea, Ship, Travel**

Walking *See* **Journeys**

Walls

✖ **Jumping over a wall** – you should be able to overcome present difficulties through sheer effort.
◆ **Falling from a wall** – prospects are not so bright.

War

◆ A sign of friction within the family or, perhaps, on the work front.
See also **Aggression, Army, Battle, Fight, Soldiers**

Warts

✖ **On your hands** – you are likely to come into money.
◆ **On others** – a sign that you suspect hostility.

Washing

◆ The person who is washing is probably feeling or should be feeling guilty.

Water

✖ ◆ It is very common to dream of water. The amount of water and the mood and circumstances of the dreamer are important in interpretation. It can mean

vigour, birth, death or cleansing (or the absence or fear of these).
See also **Flood, Lagoon, Lake, Ocean, River, Sea**

Wealth
● **Accumulation of money** – symbolic of the desire for increased knowledge and wisdom.
✖ **The wealth of others** – an indication that you have reliable friends.
See also **Bank, Gold, Millionaire, Money**

Weapons
◆ ✖ In all dreams about weapons there is a strong element of aggression and maybe even a deathwish. The mood of the dream is important. However, the aggression may be accompanied by bravery.
See also **Aggression, Guns, Knife**

Wedding
● **Dreamt by a woman** – generally a wish-fulfilment dream.
◆ **Dreamt by a man** – a deep need to resolve two opposing ideas that are bothering you.
See also **Bride, Bridegroom, Marriage**

Weight
◆ You are concerned by overwhelming troubles right now, or even, quite simply, worried about a few extra pounds you have put on. Traditionally, however, many religions put forward the idea that the soul is weighed after death or judgment. Your dream may therefore represent some concern about past behaviour.
See also **Obesity**

Wheel
✖ ◆ May refer to the wheel of fortune.
See also **Paddlewheel**

Whirlpool
◆ You feel anxious about being drawn into things against your better judgment, or are utterly confused about a present state of affairs.

Whirlwind
◆ You are anxious about the prospect of sudden change in your lifestyle.

Will
◆ **Making a will** – a sign that your subconscious is concerned that your affairs are not in order, or anxiety over how those close to you will cope after your death.
● **The reading of a will** – you seek greater recognition on the part of family and friends.
See also **Inheritance**

Wind
✖ **Light winds** – the lifeforce or transformation.
◆ **Strong winds** – an unsettling situation and perhaps anger.
See also **Storm**

Window
◆ **Closed window** – if you could not open it, you fear deep down that you are failing to communicate successfully with others.
● **Open window** – you are seeking a new way of life.
● **Idealized landscape beyond** – signifies a yearning for greater satisfaction generally.

◆ **Face at the window** – you fear criticism for some past action.

Wine

✿ **Drunk in friendly circumstances** – the omens are happy.
✚ **Combined with drunkenness** – there may be a problem with alcohol.
See also **Alcohol, Drunkenness**

Witch/wizard

◆ **Dreamer as the witch** – you are expressing repressed anger at someone.
◆ **Encounter with a witch** – you fear that someone is plotting against you.
● **On a broomstick** – sometimes taken to have sexual significance.

Words

◆ **Threats** – the dreamer's conscience is disturbed.
◆ **Bad language** – some inner problem needs looking at.
◆ **Faint words** – perhaps the dreamer has not understood or does not want to understand something.
See also **Accusation, Argument, Language, Speech**

Wounds

◆ The dreamer fears mutilation, scarring, castration, loss of virginity, impotence. Generally, it is a cry for help.

Wreck *See* **Accident, Crash, Journeys**

Writing

● **Taking pen to paper** – you seek an outlet for creativity in waking life.

◆ **Analysing someone else's handwriting** – you fear that person's motives. Take particular note of the content of the writing in your dream.
See also **Illiteracy, Letter, Words**

Wrong

◆ To be in the wrong place or at the wrong time means the dreamer has a sense of wrongdoing.

X-rays

◆ You are fearful of revealing your true, inner feelings to a loved one. Such a dream may also be a pointer to deep concerns about your own or someone else's physical health.
See also **Doctor, Hospital, Illness**

Yacht

◆ **In choppy seas** – there could be stormy times ahead.
✖ **In calm seas** – you are likely to come into money before too long.

● **Alone on a simple craft** – you are in need of a break from the pressures of daily life.
See also **Sea, Ship**

Zip

◆ ● If the zip is stuck, this is very much how you feel in waking life: in a rut and anxious for some element of change. Alternatively, your subconscious may be speaking in puns: perhaps it is saying that you really need more 'zip' or excitement in your life.

Zoo

♦ ● **Contented caged animals** – your subconscious is expressing its wish for a contented family life.

● **Frustrated caged animals** – you would dearly like to escape from some restrictive situation either at home or at work.

See also **Animals, Cage**

7. Dream diary

Being able to commit your dreams to memory is a rare
talent, since they fade as quickly as the morning frost.
You may be able to recount the dream to a friend quite
soon after waking – and, perhaps, even during the day –
but you are bound to forget it eventually. So resolve to
keep a dream diary

A TOOL FOR UNDERSTANDING

Since dreams are messages from the unconscious mind,
they shed light on the deepest of secrets. We can only
piece together some meaning from them if we can
recall them vividly enough, or see a pattern emerging
from their occurrence.

HOW TO KEEP THE DIARY

Keeping a dream diary helps you to understand yourself
more fully, and as you become more practised, it will
also become a pleasure. At first, what you remember
may be rather sketchy. But as you study your notes,
many more details will probably come to mind.
You could keep a note-pad by the bedside, writing up
each dream in a rough form immediately when you
wake. Then, later, you can transfer the information to
an 'official' dream diary, using your rough notes as a
memory aid.

Precise information

In order for your diary to serve as a practical record, you
will need to write down as much about the dream as
possible in order to study it later from different angles.
1 You should put in the day you had the dream, the

date, the time and, if recording several dreams, the
order in which the dreams occurred.

2 Describe the mood or atmosphere. These give a
strong clue to the meaning of the dream, and may linger
for hours, days or even weeks, even though the images
fade fast.

3 Put in as much detail on the content as possible.

4 Under a category called 'Additional notes', list some
of the important events that have happened within the
past day or so, and any that you look forward to. This
might help shed light on the formation of your dreams,
which inevitably incorporate elements of daytime
experiences, and of the people you meet.

USING THE DIARY FOR SELF-EXAMINATION

Soon after you start to record your dreams, you should
try to understand the way in which your mind produces
symbols (see also chapter 6). Many symbols are
produced by association – the creation of images that
are connected in the dreamer's mind with the idea or
emotion that is the real subject of the dream. Some
symbols are common to most people – for example,
water is widely associated with emotions and fire with
power.

Personal symbols

Personal associations in everyday life often occur
symbolically in dreams. For example, what do you
associate with your car or other pieces of personal
property? If you associate your car with sex, then
whenever a car appears in a dream, it symbolizes sex.
However, if your car represents a safe refuge, then it
will have that meaning in your dreams.

Aid to self-knowledge

When you look over the diary after a month, say, you could discover some significant patterns in the subject matter of your dreams. This permanent record may gain you an insight into your deepest desires and fears. You may find, for instance, that a certain repetitive dream always occurs on a Sunday night or early Monday morning, revealing your innermost feelings about the prospect of your working week.

A dream diary
- is used to record dreams before they fade
- should be done in rough notes upon waking
- will bring greater self-insight
- means recording events and mood
- should include recent past and future happenings
- might allow recognition of patterns and repeats

SAMPLE DREAM DIARIES

The examples that follow show how all the important factors can be tabulated.

Day of week Wednesday
Date 8 March 1993
Time Woke at 4.30 a.m.
Content Leave clients office.
○ Cannot remember where I
parked car. Seem to search
for hours. Then find it, but
I should not be driving as have
not passed test and have no
licence. Drive home, terrified that
police may stop me.
Mood Great anxiety
Colours Red car
Additional Notes Overwhelming
○ feeling of guilt, even though
have never knowingly broken
the law in everyday life.
Six weeks before, failed exams.

Day of week Friday
Date 10 March 1993
Time Woke at 7am.
Content Wander into a department store and up escalator.
Stand at the scarf counter and
speak to sales assistant. She is
very attractive, but when she
leans over to tie scarf around my
neck, she turns into window
dummy.
Mood Disappointment/gloom
Colours Dull, bright green scarf
Additional Notes Everyone in the
store was walking as if
underwater. Had recently met
young woman whom I was
thinking of asking out.

Day of week Sunday/Monday
Date 13 March 1993
Time Woke at 3.15 am.
Content Dreamt I was in office
staring out at magnificent
rainbow.
Expecting someone to come in and
question me about certain files.
Accountant walks past, and out
of window. Said he had to check
how much money in the bucket at
end of rainbow.
Mood Mixed-joy and concern
Colours Brilliant
Additional Notes A sense of
wonder at the beauty of the world.
But underlying worry about my
part in it. Have job interview in a
week's time

Glossary

anima/animus A figure of the opposite sex to that of the dreamer who contains some of the dreamer's characteristics. These terms are also used to convey the 'feminine' (emotional, instinctive) qualities within the man or the 'masculine' (intellectual, reflective) qualities within the woman.

archetypes According to Jung, who coined the word, these are universal symbols important in the formation of dreams. The horse, for example, represents the animal side of a person – and, therefore, the unconscious mind, which cannot be tamed. Other archetypal symbols include the mother, representing, for instance, nature, the womb, instinctive life; the shadow, or the unrecognized side of the person; the mandala, or magic circle, which represents the self and its striving for wholeness; and the creation of the world, a myth told in similar ways by many different cultures.

astral projection In esoteric lore, the astral body is an exact counterpart to the physical body, in which it is encased. Projection occurs when the astral body breaks free just before death or during certain dreams.
See also out-of-body experience.

ego (from Latin and Greek words for 'I' or 'self') According to Freud, this is the conscious self that uses logic and judgment in dealing with the world, and is guided by what he termed the 'reality principle'. The ego is supposed to keep the id under control.
See also id, superego.

electroencephalogram or EEG The graphic record of brainwaves. It is traced by an electroencephalograph, which translates electrical energy from the brain into visual patterns.

hypnogogic state The moments between waking and sleeping – when the mind begins to lose touch with daily reality. During this period, the mind sometimes conjures fleeting, hallucinatory images. The same term is now also applied to the state between sleeping and waking.

id (Latin for 'it') In Freudian theory, this is the primitive, instinctual and childish part of the personality that obeys the 'pleasure principle'.
See also ego, superego.

incubation Inducing dreams, both in ancient and modern times. The Egyptians and Greeks used to sleep overnight in a special sanctuary, hoping to incubate dreams that would contain divine answers to their problems, often about health.

lucid dream The dreamer is suddenly aware that he or she is dreaming, alerted because of something strangely inconsistent. Lucid dreams are memorably vivid. They can be induced and controlled.

near-death experience (NDE) The mind or 'soul' leaves the body and goes to a more peaceful and joyful level of existence, before rejoining the body. Near-death experiences occur during illness.
See also out-of-body experience.

noradrenaline One of two 'arousal' hormones released

by the adrenal glands – the other is adrenaline. Both trigger body changes in response to strong emotions, such as fear, anger and sexual aggression. During sleep, less noradrenaline is produced. This may be partly why people in REM sleep are especially difficult to wake. *See also* serotonin.

oracle In classical antiquity, a place where deities were consulted via priests, and the response given at such a place. Also refers to a person whose words were regarded as wise and authoritative. Petitioners often brought dreams for interpretation, though the answers were sometimes obscure and even misleading.

out-of-body experience (OBE) A sense that an individual is separated from his or her physical body, and can view it from above. Some people claim they can generate OBEs at will. Sometimes also used for 'false awakening', an illusion of having woken when still asleep and dreaming.

paradoxical sleep Another term for REM sleep – the stage of the sleep cycle associated with dreaming in which the rapid eye movements of the sleeper indicate sleep, not wakefulness.
See also REM sleep.

precognition The ability to perceive future events through the use of extrasensory perception. In dreams, it frequently concerns disasters or accidents, perhaps reflecting the dreamer's unconscious anxiety.

REM sleep The stage of light sleep especially associated with vivid dreams, recurring about every 90 minutes in the sleep cycle. Its features include rapid movement of the pupils, quick and shallow breathing and paralysis of the large body muscles (though fingers and toes may twitch).

serial dreams Continuation of a theme or story through several succeeding dreams. Some individuals are able to dream, wake up, go back to sleep and continue with the same dream.

serotonin A hormone that helps to transmit nerve impulses in the brain. One of its functions may be to regulate the work of organs during light sleep.
See also noradrenaline.

shadow One of Jung's archetypes and a figure of the same sex as the dreamer. Usually it represents the ignored part of the personality because the dreamer does not like what he or she stands for.

subconscious The part of the mind considered not fully conscious, but still able to influence action.
See also unconscious.

superego That part of the human psyche concerned with morality, so called by Freud because it is above, or superior to, the ego. Freud regarded this as the third part of the personality.
See also ego, id.

symbol In the dream world – and in daily life – these are objects that are representative of something else and have a special meaning. In interpreting dreams, it is important to analyse their symbolic content, since the unconscious usually speaks to us through symbols.

unconscious That part of the mind, according to
Freud, that contains all the memories of childhood
including the instincts and emotions forgotten by the
conscious mind. Jung, however, thought there were two
parts to the unconscious: the personal unconscious
(half-remembered thoughts or ideas that constitute a
'complex'), and the collective unconscious, containing
'racial memories' – shared myths and stories – with
which each of us is supposedly born.
See also subconscious.

Index

COLLINS GEM

BABIES' names
a ? z

• a mine of information

COLLINS GEM

BEER

• a mine of information

COLLINS GEM

BIRDS

• a mine of information

COLLINS GEM

CALORIE Counter

• a mine of information

COLLINS GEM

FACT FILE

• a mine of information

COLLINS GEM

FENG SHUI

• a mine of information

COLLINS GEM

FLAGS

• a mine of information

COLLINS GEM

Healthy **EATING**

• a mine of information

COLLINS GEM

QUOTATIONS

• a mine of information

COLLINS GEM

SAS Self-Defence

• a mine of information

COLLINS GEM

SAS Survival Guide

• a mine of information

COLLINS GEM

SEASHORE

• a mine of information

COLLINS GEM

TREES

• a mine of information

COLLINS GEM

Understanding **DREAMS**

• a mine of information

COLLINS GEM

WILD flowers

• a mine of information

COLLINS GEM

WINE Dictionary

• a mine of information